UNDERSTANDING

JOSEPH HELLER

Understanding Contemporary
American Literature

Matthew J. Bruccoli, *Editor*

UNDERSTANDING

Joseph

HELLER

SANFORD PINSKER

UNIVERSITY OF SOUTH CAROLINA PRESS

The author wishes to thank the following publishers for permission to reprint the designated selections. Rights in all cases are reserved by the owner of the copyright:

From *Catch-22* by Joseph Heller © 1961, and from *Good as Gold* by Joseph Heller © 1979, both reprinted by permission of the publisher, Simon & Schuster, Inc. From *Something Happened* by Joseph Heller © 1974, and from *God Knows* by Joseph Heller © 1984, both reprinted by permission of the publisher, Alfred A. Knopf Inc. From *No Laughing Matter* by Joseph Heller and Speed Vogel © 1986, and from *Picture This* by Joseph Heller © 1988, both reprinted by permission of the Putnam Publishing Group.

Published in Columbia, South Carolina, by the
University of South Carolina Press

Manufactured in the United States of America

Library of Congress Cataloging-in-Publication Data

Pinsker, Sanford.
　　Understanding Joseph Heller / Sanford Pinsker.
　　　　p.　　cm. — (Understanding contemporary American literature)
　　Includes bibliographical references and index.
　　ISBN 0-87249-751-8 (hard cover : acid free)
　　1. Heller, Joseph—Criticism and interpretation.　I. Title.
　II. Series.
　PS3558.E476Z82　　　1991
　813′.54—dc20　　　　　　　　　　　　　　　　　90-28930
　　　　　　　　　　　　　　　　　　　　　　　　　　　　CIP

CONTENTS

EDITOR'S PREFACE

Understanding Contemporary American Literature has been planned as a series of guides or companions for students as well as good nonacademic readers. The editor and publisher perceive a need for these volumes because much of the influential contemporary literature makes special demands. Uninitiated readers encounter difficulty in approaching works that depart from the traditional forms and techniques of prose and poetry. Literature relies on conventions, but the conventions keep evolving; new writers form their own conventions—which in time may become familiar. Put simply, *UCAL* provides instruction in how to read certain contemporary writers—identifying and explicating their material, themes, use of language, point of view, structures, symbolism, and responses to experience.

The word *understanding* in the series title was deliberately chosen. Many willing readers lack an adequate understanding of how contemporary literature works; that is, what the author is attempting to express and the means by which it is conveyed. Although the level of criticism and analysis in the series has been aimed at a level of general accessibility, these introductory volumes are meant to be applied in conjunction with the works they cover. Thus they do not provide a substitute for the works and authors they introduce, but rather prepare the reader for more profitable literary experiences.

M.J.B.

ACKNOWLEDGMENTS

I would like to acknowledge the generous help provided by Franklin and Marshall College, by my colleagues and students in the Department of English, and especially by my research assistant on this project, Michael Harmatz. Whatever the "catches" in the pages that follow, and whatever their number, the faults are mine alone.

UNDERSTANDING

JOSEPH HELLER

CHAPTER ONE

Understanding
Joseph Heller

Career

Joseph Heller grew up in the Coney Island section of Brooklyn, New York, a world tough enough to make him street-wise and yet vibrant enough for him to remember childhood fondly: "I cannot imagine a better place for a child to grow up in."[1] Like many other Jewish immigrants Heller's father had fled Czarist Russia, arriving in America in 1913. He drove a delivery truck for Messinger's bakery, but died—as the result of a botched operation—when Heller was five years old. At the time the young Heller did not grasp the full impact of what had happened, but readers of his adult fiction can recognize the effects. As Heller puts it, "I didn't realize then how traumatized I was."[2]

At the same time, however, there was a considerable difference between the easygoing, essentially secular, American-Jewishness of the Heller household and the neurotic, psychologically crippling childhood that Philip Roth associates with growing up Jewish in Newark, New Jersey. For Heller "closeness" was a literal fact of apartment life in Brighton Beach's immigrant Jewish neighborhood, and the Coney Island fairgrounds bustled with barkers and assorted low-grade hucksters:

> Later we came upon a . . . principle that trained us toward cynicism, the fact that it is often impossible to obtain fair value. We learned this from the barkers who offered to guess your weight, guess your name or occupation, the part of the country you came from or the date you were born, guess anything at all about you for a dime, a quarter, a half-dollar or a dollar, because here was a setup where the customer could never win.[3]

Here, writ small, are the double binds, the Catch-22's, the entrapments variously represented in Heller's fiction by military regulations, corporate bureaucracies, or political machines.

Heller's formal education included Coney Island's P.S. 188 and Abraham Lincoln High School. After he graduated from the latter in 1941, he worked as a blacksmith's helper and as a shipping file clerk for a casualty insurance company (shades of the young Bob Slocum of Heller's second novel, *Something Happened*), before enlisting in the air force the following year.

Heller's military experiences are simultaneously reflected and comically exaggerated in *Catch-22*. From May 1944 to mid-1945 he was stationed on Corsica with the 488th Squadron of the 340th Bombardment Group. Heller flew sixty combat missions as a bombardier, earning the Air Medal, a presidential unit citation, and eventually a promotion to lieutenant. In large measure the war was winding down by the time Heller arrived overseas; enemy air strikes were uncommon, and much of his tour of duty could be described as "easy time"—playing baseball or basketball with fellow aviators or simply whiling away the long stretches between bombing missions.

There was, however, one exception to Heller's idyllic time on Corsica. On his thirty-seventh mission—flying over Avignon—Heller suddenly realized that war is a game in which one's opponents are out to kill you. A member of his crew was critically wounded, and once again the Death Question had to be taken into full account. In *Catch-22* Heller would return, again and again, to the specter of Snowden slowly dying in Yossarian's arms.

After the war Heller met and married Shirley Held. He also enrolled in the University of Southern California under the GI Bill, but was soon persuaded to transfer to New York University by Whit Burnett, his mentor and editor of *Story* magazine. Heller graduated Phi Beta Kappa in 1948. During the next academic year he began his studies for an MA in English at Columbia University, taking, among others, a course in American literature taught by the eminent critic Lionel Trilling.

In 1949 Heller won a Fulbright and spent the next year at St. Catherine's College, Oxford, presumably reading for a BA degree. Although he read deeply in Chaucer, Shakespeare, and Milton—and by all accounts was making good progress—his serious work went into the writing of short stories.

Nonetheless, by 1950 Heller had become sufficiently informed about literature and literary study to get a job in Penn State's English composition program. His heavy Brooklyn accent and urban style no doubt contributed to whatever legacies of alienation he brought with him. In any event, he left Penn State two years later, and with the exception of limited stints teaching creative writing at Yale University and the City University of New York

(CUNY), he has shown little inclination to return to academe's groves.

From 1952 to 1956 Heller worked as an advertising copywriter for *Time* (the organization, Heller once told an interviewer, that also employs the Bob Slocum of *Something Happened*), and then served as a promotion manager at *McCall's* from 1958 to 1961.

All the while, of course, Heller was working on his own writing—first, a series of unrelated short stories, a few movie and television scripts under the pseudonym Max Orange, and then a long novel that he called "Catch-18." "I Don't Love You Any More," published in Whit Burnett's *Story* magazine, was followed by four short stories—two in *Atlantic Monthly*, two in *Esquire*—all during 1948.

But successful though Heller was as a short-story writer, it was the section of his novel-in-progress that appeared in *New World Writing* 7 (1955) which made the difference. Here was fiction not only unlike his earlier stories but also unlike anything one could remember reading. The selection had daring, dark humor, dazzling experimentation, and best of all, a distinctive voice.

Six years later the novel itself—now called *Catch-22*—appeared. Some of its earliest reviewers did not shower it with adulation. Writing in *The New Yorker*, Whitney Balliett complained that "it doesn't even seem to have been written: instead it gives the impression of having been shouted onto paper."[4] But others—including novelists Nelson Algren and Thomas Pynchon—were enthusiastic in their praise. If *A Farewell to Arms* and *All Quiet on the Western Front* defined the initiation and disillusionment that marked the essential differences between literature about previous warfare and the literature about World

War I, *Catch-22* explored the ways a novel about World War II might not only avoid duplicating the formulas of a novel such as Norman Mailer's *The Naked and the Dead*, but also come closer to the truth of war itself.

Heller chose to concentrate on issues of survival rather than on initiation and to see the military bureaucracy and its absurd logic—symbolized by "Catch-22"—as greater threats than Nazi gunfire. In this sense *Catch-22* is as much a parody of the war novel as it is a war novel per se; in other respects it is a war novel only by the accidents of time and place, of plot outline and superficial circumstance. For *Catch-22* tells readers more, much more, about the unexamined, overly organized life in corporate America than it does about World War II.

Nonetheless, for those protesting the war in Vietnam and in search of a metaphor equal to the absurdities that escalated along with America's military involvement, *Catch-22* became the novel of choice. It struck just the right notes—at once loopy and antiestablishment—for those countercultural times. No matter that *Catch-22* is no more "about" the war in Vietnam than it was "about" the last months of the Italian campaign; Heller had touched a nerve, and the novel found no end of critics with close readings of its form and theories about its function.

Meanwhile, the love affair with Heller's first novel continued, as sales hit the ten million mark on its twenty-fifth anniversary, and "catch-22" elbowed its way into the language and then into *Webster's New World Dictionary of the American Language* (1970): "a paradox in law, regulation, or practice that makes one a victim of its provisions no matter what one does."

Given a debut of such dizzying proportions, Heller's next venture—a play with the prophetic title *We Bombed in New Haven* (1968)—could only be a let-down, if not quite the unmitigated disaster, the "bomb," that some reviewers made of it. For all its absurdist touches in the manner of Edward Albee, for all its strained surrealism, the play is an exercise in antiwar preaching and, as such, it preaches to the choir. Those anxious to number themselves among the angels were quick to point out the devastating ironies in Captain Starkey's insistence that "there has never been a war, . . . nobody has been killed here tonight"—this, after sending his own son to a certain death—but those who felt that the drama should *dramatize* its point were neither amused nor convinced. The play closed after eighty-six performances, more a testimony to Heller's growing reputation as the author of *Catch-22* than to his powers as a playwright.

Heller's second novel—*Something Happened* (1974)—made it clear, however, that he was indeed a novelist to be reckoned with. No doubt *Catch-22* will remain the novel most associated with Heller, but many critics would argue that *Something Happened* is the more disturbing, and the richer, book.

Bob Slocum, the novel's first-person narrator, is an extended portrait of the corporate world and its ability to deaden one's moral sensibilities. If innocence energizes the Yossarian of *Catch-22*, experience makes Slocum by turns cynical and world-weary, anxious and paranoid. He *speaks*, rather than "writes," his tale of how he was metamorphosed into a contemporary version of Everyman, a creature resigned to his sufferings at the office and his inadequacies at home. Apparently "something happened" when Slocum was young and put in time as a file clerk, but unlike Snowden's "secret"—that man is matter, and that he can be blown apart by enemy gunfire—

Slocum can never quite find, much less touch, his formative wound.

Heller's next novel, *Good as Gold* (1979), was also built upon a premise of great expectations coupled with absurdist disappointment. Professor Bruce Gold hopes that a contract—and a healthy advance—to write a book about the American-Jewish experience will put his financial affairs, and his life, into some order. In this sense he resembles Moses Herzog, Saul Bellow's brainy but distracted protagonist. Like Herzog, Gold can think up projects faster than he can write manuscript pages. But *Good as Gold* suffers from its own excesses, from its inability to decide if it is going to be a satire of American-Jewish life largely played out at the Gold family dinner table, a send-up of the Washington bureaucracy and its endless capacity for double-talk (throughout the novel Gold twists in the wind as everything from an ''unnamed source'' to a possible Secretary of State), or a diatribe directed at Henry Kissinger. Sprawl has always been Heller's identifying characteristic, but *Good as Gold* is a case where its liabilities outweighed its assets.

Much the same thing can be said of *God Knows* (1984), Heller's attempt to yoke the story of David with the *shtick* of a Borscht Belt comic. King David's insistence that his story has more literary dimension, more conflict, more sheer *style* than the other books of the Bible speaks to his sense of justice thwarted, to his conviction that he has been misunderstood by history. The result is something akin to ''The Bible According to Joseph Heller''—an irreverent, often hilarious romp through the books of Chronicles and Samuel.

No Laughing Matter (1986), written with alternating chapters by his friend Speed Vogel, is a nonfictional treatment of Heller's bout with Guillain-Barré syndrome and how the old gang (Mario Puzo, Mel Brooks, Julius Green) rallied round. Heller has hardly been shy about drawing fictional portraits from life experiences, but this time autobiography is all.

Heller's most recent novel, *Picture This* (1988), is an extended exercise in deconstruction, one that begins by "contemplating" Rembrandt's famous painting *Aristotle Contemplating the Bust of Homer* and ends by dismantling its component parts. At issue are not only the blurring lines that separate illusion from reality, art from life, but also what the greed and crimes of history have to say about our own time. On these points Heller can, and does, become tedious. Nonetheless, *Picture This* has touches that remind readers of Heller's style at its satiric best. No doubt these same readers will look forward to the sequel of *Catch-22* that Heller keeps promising, but until that day there is a considerable body of work worthy of their attention and their thought.

Overview

Joseph Heller's fiction has a nervous, anxious edge, as if the world, and especially its language, is shifting so rapidly, so absurdly, that any discoveries a protagonist might make are not likely to come in time. As the "lessons" of *Picture This* try to demonstrate, only names and places change; history itself repeats itself in a relentless saga of political machination and private scheming, of pointless wars and meaningless deaths. Into the teeth of the world's storms Heller hurls one-liners.

Disorder is, in short, the order of the day. Ordinary citizens are victimized not so much by bureaucratic rules as by the rule of bureaucracy. Or to alter Lord Acton's formula, authority corrupts, and absolute authority corrupts absolutely. Heller chronicles the abuses—whether they occur on the battlefield or in corporate board rooms—with bemused contempt. Bubbling just underneath the amazement, however, is a satiric indictment of systems so familiar, so logical in their illogic, that we accept the absurdities as "normal."

Because *Catch-22* so dominates contemporary thinking about Heller, it is hardly surprising that he strikes critics as a death-haunted, death-obsessed novelist. Indeed, there are too many dangers in *Catch-22*, too many potential murderers and too many likely perils for Yossarian to keep track of them all. Nonetheless, he tries to account for the major menaces, and the result is a darkly comic listing that reveals as much about Heller's style as it does about the shivery condition of Heller's world:

There was Hitler, Mussolini and Tojo, for example, and they were all out to kill him. There was Lieutenant Scheisskopf with his fanaticism for parades and there was the bloated colonel with his big fat mustache and his fanaticism for retribution, and they wanted to kill him, too. There was Appleby, Havermeyer, Black and Korn. There was Nurse Cramer and Nurse Duckett, who he was almost certain wanted him dead, and there was the Texan and the C.I.D. man, about whom he had no doubt. There were bartenders, bricklayers, and bus conductors all over the world who wanted him dead, landlords and tenants, traitors and patriots, lynchers, leeches and lackeys, and they were all out to bump him off. That was the secret Snowden had spilled to him on the mission to Avignon—they were out to get him; and Snowden had spilled it all over the back of the plane.[5]

Put simply, Yossarian wants to know *why*. What he discovers, of course, is that nothing can be put simply, and that even though the war's outcome is no longer in doubt, the number of bombing missions keeps multiplying. In a world where commanders worry about "tight bomb clusters," where a man named Major Major is given a commission because the possibilities of a Major Major Major are too good to pass up, where the fine print of air force regulations can be as deadly as enemy flak, Yossarian wants, above all else, to *survive*.

An obsession with what Saul Bellow has called the "Death Question" need not, however, take such surrealistic turns. In *Something Happened*, for example, Bob Slocum tries desperately to avoid stumbling into evidences of the Grim Reaper's handiwork, but his is a case of ignorance breeding anxieties rather than bliss. The very fact that Slocum doesn't *want* to know reinforces the fear that the unknown breeds.

> When police cars collect, I don't want to know why, although I'm glad they've arrived and hope they've come in time to do what they've been called to do. When an ambulance comes, I'd rather not know for whom. And when children drown, choke, or are killed by automobiles or trains, I don't want to know which children they are, because I'm always afraid they might turn out to be mine.
>
> I have a similar aversion to hospitals and the same misgivings and distaste for people I know who fall

ill. . . . When friends, relatives, and business acquaintances are stricken with heart attacks now, I never call the hospital or hospital room to find out how they are, because there's always the danger I might find out they are dead. . . . This sometimes strains relationships (even with my wife, who is always asking everybody how they are and running to hospitals with gifts to visit people who are there), but I can't care. I just don't want to talk to people whose husband or father or wife or mother or child may be dying, even though the dying person himself might be someone I feel deeply attached to. I never want to find out that anybody I know is dead.[6]

That a writer so given to grisly descriptions of the dead and dying, the sick and the sickly, should find himself the victim of Guillain-Barré syndrome is an irony that only a Heller could fully appreciate—especially when a world-class hypochondriac and *tummler* such as Mel Brooks pays a "sick call"—and that only a Heller could turn into the stuff of *No Laughing Matter*.

Nonetheless, Heller's canon is not the endless cataloging of bizarre deaths that his readers imagine. Language misused or misappropriated, language debased and debunked, figures much more prominently in the long arc of his career. Consider, for example, this representative exchange from *Good as Gold*:

"Oh, yes," Ralph assured him. "It's always like this when it's this way."

Gold succeeded in speaking without sarcasm. "How is it when it isn't?"

"Isn't what, Bruce?"

"This way."

"Different."

"In what way, Ralph?"

"In different ways, Bruce, unless they're the same, in which case it's this way."

"Ralph," Gold had to ask, "don't people here laugh or smile when you talk that way?"

"What way, Bruce?"

"You seem to qualify or contradict all your statements."

"Do I?" Ralph considered the matter intently. "Maybe I do seem a bit oxymoronic at times. I think everyone here talks that way."[7]

As Gold soon discovers, everyone in the Washington bureaucracy does indeed talk precisely this way. Disorder is the political animal's natural order; obfuscation comes with the territory of internal memos and press releases. For Heller the result more closely approximates Theater of the Absurd—say, Eugene Ionesco's *The Bald Soprano*—than *politics* as Aristotle defined the term. "No one governs," Gold observes. "Everyone performs. Politics has become a social world." And indeed the widely disparate social worlds that Heller's novels explore—World War II's Italian front, corporate America, biblical Judea, classical Athens, or seventeenth-century Holland—count finally for less than Heller's dark, satirical conviction that language *is* power, that language *is* what passes for reality, and that the Real and the Rational have, at best, a slim chance for a hearing. Come up with the right phrase—whether it be "catch-22" or "mind-boggling"—and the world snaps to attention.

In *The Waste Land* T. S. Eliot makes a case for seeing the London of his day as an "unreal city," cut off from sources of myth and culture that had once given vitality to the past. Heller is too street-smart, too cynical, too much the absurdist, to put much stock in visions of a Golden Age. He prefers instead to think of the sweep of civilization as "unreal," and history itself as the story of man's linguistic inhumanity to man. In short, what goes around comes around—as Heraclitus and Vico, contemporary slang and the "soldier in white" know all too well:

> The soldier in white was encased from head to toe in plaster and gauze. He had two useless legs and two useless arms. He had been smuggled into the ward during the night, and the men had no idea he was among them until they awoke in the morning and saw the two strange legs hoisted from the hips, the two strange arms anchored up perpendicularly, all four limbs pinioned strangely in air by lead weights suspended darkly above him that never moved. Sewn into the bandages over the insides of both elbows were zippered lips through which he was fed clear fluid from a clear jar. A silent zinc pipe rose from the cement on his groin and was coupled to a slim rubber hose that carried waste from his kidneys and dripped it efficiently into a clear, stoppered jar on the floor. When the jar on the floor was full, the jar feeding his elbow was empty, and the two were simply switched quickly so that stuff could drip back into him. All they ever really saw of the soldier in white was a frayed black hole over his mouth.[8]

The world teaches protagonists such as Yossarian and Bruce Gold hard lessons—namely, that slogans of progress are a lie, and that progress is an illusion. Once caught up in the nets of language that those in power wield, one can only thrash about helplessly. Words simply will not stand still. As Frederick R. Karl rightly points out,

> Heller often works by defining or suggesting elements through the negative. His entire novel [*Catch-22*] is an expanded litotes, that form of understatement and irony in which something is expressed by way of the negative of its opposite. Litotes is, also, a form of wit. One never says "not many" but says "not a few," creating a dialectical confusion as to how many or how few. "Catch-22" as a phrase which has entered the language is connected to its litotic function. For it expresses an underlining negative aspect: if you are crazy, you need not fly, but if you do not want to fly, that proves you're not crazy. The expression upsets our notions of what is, what is not, in the way a comic uses wit to express the opposite of what we ordinarily take for granted.[9]

In similar ways Bruce Gold finds himself embroiled in worlds where terms are so balanced that they cancel each other out; for a writer—and especially one as ambitious and as naïve as Gold—the result is to pile one confusion upon another until he strikes paydirt. The right turn of phrase, however meaningless, might just do the trick. Unfortunately, Gold fares no better than other Heller protagonists. Like the number of bombing missions that always climbs just out of reach, Gold finds himself being "hoped" to death.

In Heller's fictive world a protagonist's persistent complaint often boils down to this: *Who's got the story?* And if the worry afflicts a Yossarian at the receiving end of

Understanding Joseph Heller

Catch-22's insidious, death-dealing blows or a Bruce Gold trying to tiptoe his way across the linguistic minefields that line Pennsylvania Avenue, it also bothers those uneasy regal heads upon which crowns rest. King David—the slayer of Goliath, psalmist *extraordinaire*, and the character with what he insists is "the best story in the Bible"—is hardly an exception. Indeed, the more he thinks about his life, the more he concludes that the biblical account doesn't do him justice. After all, he protests,

> I think I had a nobler subject in Saul and Jonathan than he did in Sampson, that crude, blundering jackass who bullied his parents into arranging marriages they disapproved of. . . . A *naar* like him they make a Judge, while I don't even have one book in the Bible named after me. What really gets my goat is that Samuel has I and II, even though he dies in I and doesn't get a single mention in II, not one. Is that fair? And those two books of Samuel should be named for me, not for him. What's so great about Samuel?[10]

Ironically enough, the dynamics of protest change when the clutches of Guillain-Barré syndrome—a mysterious, debilitating condition that attacks the central nervous system—force Heller to turn his absurdist humor inward. His protagonists may have bad cases of what Bob Slocum calls "the willies," and they may feel, like King David, that they are at the mercy of other people's stories about them, but one always had the sense that Heller was behind the scenes, fully in charge. After all, *story* is what a writer controls; it is his "power" in a world that too often defines the term in the doublespeak of corporate memos or administrative policy. None of this, however, applies to those who suffer from Guillain-Barré syndrome. Suddenly

Heller—as writer, as literary personality, as bon vivant—is rendered powerless, helpless, dependent.

To be sure, *No Laughing Matter* is hardly as grim a book as the description above might make it sound. But the very fact that Heller alternates his chapters with those written by Speed Vogel suggests a new condition, one in which important aspects of his "story" are consigned to a perspective other than his own.

Granted, *No Laughing Matter* is an exception. When his affliction disappears as mysteriously as it had arrived, Heller returns to his old post at the helm of "story." Moreover, he returns with what can only be called a historical vengeance, as he casts a sourly imperial view over the sweep of man's cruelty to man. It is at once an easy posture to assume and one that grows increasingly complicated, endlessly embroidered, in the telling. But one thing, at least, is clear: Heller has the *story*, which is to say, the "goods," on what makes for war as well as art.

Heller can be written down as a social satirist, as one who comments ironically on a world that most people accept too quickly and too unthinkingly. But that characterization, however correct, misses the fiercely prophetic note that lies just behind his protagonists' befuddlements. For Heller's attacks on the body politic, on corporate bureaucracy, on the machinery of war as well as the machineries of domestic life, have the look of a jeremiad. In short, Heller can be numbered among those who bring the comfortable and complacent "bad news" about their lives. When his fiction is working most successfully—as it is in *Catch-22* and *Something Happened*—ironic distancing and black humor keep message and medium at a delicate balance; when the vehicle works less successfully (as is the case with *Picture This*), one gets the point without also getting the traditional satisfactions that well-wrought fictions give.

Heller learned early, and painfully, that life has a nasty habit of throwing spitballs and then of covering over the infractions with layers of doublespeak. His fiction provides a way both of patterning and of controlling a chaotic universe, one in which the possibilities of an old-fashioned heroism have been gradually eroded. Nonetheless, his protagonists, like the zany versions of Kafka's Joseph K. that they are, manage to persist, to force their antagonists into darkly comic dialogues, and even, at moments, to effect versions of triumph. To say that Heller strikes many readers as the quintessentially contemporary American man is to belabor the obvious. He is that, and he is much, much more. He is, for example, among contemporary American literature's most accomplished, most dazzling stylists, and a writer who has put his undeniable stamp on the landscape of his generation's best fiction.

NOTES

1. Heller, "Coney Island: The Fun Is Over," *Show* 10 (July 1962): 51.

2. "Coney Island" 53.

3. "Coney Island" 102.

4. Whitney Balliett, "Mrs. Jolly and Mrs. Flack," *The New Yorker* 9 Dec. 1961: 247.

5. Heller, *Catch-22* (New York: Simon and Schuster, 1961) 176–77.

6. Heller, *Something Happened* (New York: Knopf, 1974) 4–5.

7. Heller, *Good as Gold* (New York: Simon and Schuster, 1979) 122.

8. *Catch-22* 10.

9. Frederick R. Karl, *American Fictions: 1940–1980* (New York: Harper, 1983) 310.

10. Joseph Heller, *God Knows* (New York: Knopf, 1984) 31.

CHAPTER TWO

Catch-22

For Heller a novel generally begins not with a structure, an intricate plan or "plot" to be worked out, but with a sentence, one that simply popped into his head and then rattled around there, haunting him. *Catch-22* begins not only in medias res—in the middle of things—but also in something akin to wonderment: "It was love at first sight."[1] Heller's readers often feel the same way; they fall in love with the novel's playful sense of the absurd, with the way Yossarian shapes up as a rebel out to outfox the system.

Readers first meet Heller's aviator-protagonist in the infirmary rather than the wild blue yonder. Yossarian is afflicted by a pain in his liver that falls "short of being jaundice" (7) but at the same time is sufficiently puzzling to require extended hospitalization. Presumably the doctors could deal with jaundice, and they could certainly return him to active duty if it were *not* jaundice, but "this just being short of jaundice all the time confused them." To the military bureaucracy Yossarian's liver is both a puzzlement and an aggravation; and as the novel unfolds, the same things might be said of Yossarian himself.

Nothing, of course, unsettles rigid bureaucratic minds more than an aberration lodging stubbornly "between the cracks" and just beyond the grip of rules. Yossarian's case of near-jaundice is a tiny example; Yossarian himself is a much larger one. He spends as much time as possible in the hospital, not only because the meals are better there or because he can flirt with the nurses, but mostly because there he is *safe*.

Yossarian enters the world of his novel knowing what the protagonists of earlier war novels such as Erich Maria Remarque's *All Quiet on the Western Front* (1929) or Ernest Hemingway's *A Farewell to Arms* (1929) soon discover; namely, that the life of a combat soldier is nasty, brutish, and likely to be very, very short. Heller's protagonist has even fewer illusions about the patriotic rhetoric of recruitment posters or about the "romantic" character of war. He seeks out pockets of safety because he wants, above all else, to survive. As he tells Clevinger, a character whose principles are matched only by the mindless passion with which he holds them, "They're trying to kill me" (17). Not surprisingly, Clevinger, who points out that "they're shooting at *everyone*," concludes that Yossarian is "crazy." Clevinger's opinion is widely shared by those who come to hate and fear Yossarian's increasingly desperate efforts to survive; for them war is not only necessary but, more important, also perfectly sane, and those who throw monkey wrenches into its bureaucratic machinery must by definition be crazy.

Indeed, *crazy* is one of the novel's "charged words," symptomatic of a world neatly divided into the one character (Yossarian) whose sanity renders him suspect and the others whose versions of craziness are regarded as sane. Smiling down on such a world—one in which aerial photographs of "tight bombing clusters" count for more than hits or misses, or where a precision drill team has its hands surgically removed so that their commanding officer can shout "Look . . . No hands!" as they swing past in parade review—is, of course, the overarching absurdity of Catch-22 itself:

> There was only one catch and that was Catch-22, which specified that a concern for one's own safety in the face of dangers that were real and immediate was the process of a rational mind. Orr was crazy and could be grounded. All he had to do was ask; and as soon as he did, he would no longer be crazy and would have to fly more missions. Orr would be crazy to fly more missions and sane if he didn't, but if he was sane he had to fly them. If he flew them he was crazy and didn't have to; but if he didn't want to he was sane and had to. Yossarian was moved very deeply by the absolute simplicity of this clause of Catch-22 and let out a respectful whistle.
>
> "That's some catch, that Catch-22," he observed.
>
> "It's the best there is," Doc Daneeka agreed (47).

Granted, this is akin to the "logic" that reigns in Lewis Carroll's *Alice in Wonderland* rather than in conventional war novels, but that is precisely Heller's point: wars can no longer be described as "hell"; they are irrational, absurd, and in most important respects differ very little from the bureaucratic life citizens and employees experience regularly in peacetime. War merely writes the lessons of Catch-22 in starker print.

Paul Fussell's recent nonfiction book *Wartime* (1989) suggests that there may have been more affinities between

Heller's art and the "real war" than many had realized. The usual line of argument about *Catch-22* (one often encouraged by Heller himself) was that World War II, its ostensible subject, is a veiled metaphor for first the Vietnam war and then for the larger absurdities of the military-industrial complex. Perhaps so, but as Fussell points out, the "truth" about World War II—as it was lived in the foxholes and reflected in memoirs—is not at variance with his research. As he argues:

> What was it about the Second World War that moved the troops to constant verbal subversion and contempt? What was it that made the Americans, especially, so fertile with insult and cynicism, calling women Marines BAMS (broad-assed Marines) and devising SNAFU, with its offspring TARFU ("Things are really fucked up"), FUBAR ("Fucked up beyond all recognition") and the perhaps less satisfying FUBB ("Fucked up beyond belief")? It was not just the danger and fear, the boredom and uncertainty and loneliness and deprivation. It was the conviction that optimistic publicity and euphemism had rendered their experience so falsely that it would never be readily communicable. They knew that in its representation to the laity, what was happening to them was systematically sanitized and Norman Rockwellized, not to mention Disneyfied.[2]

Yossarian, then, is the man who tries desperately to bring his brand of "good news"—and a sense of Fussell's "truth"—to those still dwelling in the darkness of Plato's cave. His curious name earmarks him as an outsider and a potentially subversive character. Heller initially imagined Yossarian as an Assyrian, someone even more marginal, historically and culturally, than the Jew who generally fulfills this role in traditional war novels—only to discover later that Yossarian is an Armenian name. No matter, however, for *Yossarian* sticks in one's memory, rather like his unpredictable behaviors stick in the craw of his superiors.

Yossarian is simultaneously an enigma and an Everyman, the rebel whose bizarre behaviors unsettle and a thoroughly representative figure of the soldier's plight. What gives him both distinction and style, however, are the comic lengths to which he will go to pursue the folly of his version of the truth. For example, Yossarian's idea of a good joke is to write letters to everyone he knows telling them that he is going on a dangerous mission: " 'They asked for volunteers. It's very dangerous, but someone has to do it. I'll write you the instant I get back.' And he had not written anyone since" (8). Forced to censor the letters of enlisted men while he is confined to the hospital, Yossarian soon discovers that their lives are only slightly more interesting than his and that the chore is as monotonous as it is boring. So he gives his task a darkly imaginative twist, one emblematic of what might be called the Yossarian syndrome:

> To break the monotony he invented games. Death to all modifiers, he declared one day, and out of every letter that passed through his hands went every adverb and every adjective. The next day he made war on articles. He reached a much higher plane of creativity the following day when he blacked out everything in the letters but *a, an,* and *the*. That erected more dynamic intralinear tensions, he felt, and in just about every case left a message far more universal (8).

No doubt there are contemporary literary critics who would insist that Yossarian's linguistic games speak to the capacity of language to cancel itself out, indeed, to the impossibility of meaning itself. And other critics, more persuaded by the tragic rhythms of history, would remind Heller that World War II—Fussell's study notwithstanding—was waged to halt the spread of fascism's ugliest, most inhuman face. In *Catch-22* boredom is a bigger enemy than the Nazis; social critics are not likely to agree either with Heller's assessment or with his moral judgment.

Yossarian, of course, sees his games as versions of protest, as efforts—however minuscule, however desperate, however ineffectual—to assert the claims of the individual against those of the Machine. Given the excesses stacked on the side of the latter, it is hardly surprising that there should be a certain amount of excess on behalf of the former. Indeed, *Catch-22* thrives on excess (perhaps too much so), and this includes Yossarian's efforts to gum up semiofficial communications. Those in the know—e.g., ex-PFC Wintergreen—know better; they chuck those memos that strike them as "prolix" into the wastebaskets and thus end up wielding more *real* power than the officially powerful. By contrast Yossarian is simply playful. For example, in one letter he blacks out everything but its salutation, "Dear Mary," and then adds a closing of his own design: "I yearn for you tragically. A. T. Tappman, Chaplain, U.S. Army." Chaplain Tappman strikes Yossarian's ear as having a nice ring. Other pen names appeal to him because he can alternate the position of first and last name, as is the case with Washington Irving and Irving Washington. Washington Irving, the author of *The Sketch Book of Geoffrey Crayon, Gent.*, is one of those names that students of American literary history must dutifully remember. But he is more widely recognized as the author of "Rip Van Winkle" and "The Legend of Sleepy Hollow," two of *The Sketch Books*'s most famous pieces and early examples of what would become a staple ingredient of American humor—the tall tale.

Catch-22 is filled with stretchers and leg-pulls, with outrageous yarns told in poker face. What else is the saga of the LePage Glue Gun (which can ominously attach a whole squadron of fighter planes together and thus bring them crashing to the ground) but a yarn in the best tradition of the Old Southwest? And where else could a single aviator's moans (during a briefing) turn so contagious, eventually rising to a deafening, collective crescendo? The rub, of course, is that Yossarian's superiors take their absurdities seriously. They confuse the fatuous with the profound, but Heller's readers—as beneficiaries of the dramatic ironies he so generously heaps up—do not. Thus, Colonel Cargill, a man who has singlehandedly raised the cliché to new dizzying heights, puts it this way: "Men. . . . You're American officers. The officers of no other army in the world can make that statement. Think about it" (28). Heller's readers do, and split their sides laughing.

Meanwhile, Heller provides this deadpan account of Cargill's absurd biography, presumably by way of explaining how he came to speak as he does:

> Colonel Cargill, General Peckem's troubleshooter, was a forceful, ruddy man. Before the war he had been an alert, hard-hitting, aggressive marketing executive. He was a very bad marketing executive. Colonel Cargill was so awful a marketing executive that his services

were much sought after by firms eager to establish losses for tax purposes. Throughout the civilized world from Battery Park to Fulton Street, he was known as a dependable man for a fast tax write-off. . . . Colonel Cargill could be relied on to run the most prosperous enterprise into the ground. He was a self-made man who owed his lack of success to nobody (28).

Such minor characters (there are dozens of them) give *Catch-22* its peculiar flavor—its bulk, its texture, its richness. Many are introduced by quick brushstrokes of biography akin to the profiles that appear regularly in John Dos Passos' *USA* trilogy, but Heller throws in so many curve balls, so many absurdist contradictions, that the result is laughter. Like most great humorists, his premises are disarmingly simple (in this case he turns clichés on their heads so that Colonel Cargill starts at the top and works his way down), but his extended executions are verbally brilliant. Here, for example, is how he introduces Clevinger, a character so smart, so believing, so much the Boy Scout, that he is a dope:

As a Harvard undergraduate he had won prizes in scholarship for just about everything, and the only reason he had not won prizes in scholarship for everything else was that he was too busy signing petitions, circulating petitions and challenging petitions, joining discussion groups and resigning from discussion groups, attending youth congresses, picketing other youth congresses and organizing student committees in defense of dismissed faculty members. Everyone agreed that Clevinger was certain to go far in the academic world. In short, Clevinger was one of those people with lots of intelligence and no brains, and everyone knew it except those who soon found it out (69–70).

Subsequent biographies in *Catch-22* are cut from the same absurdist cloth that gave us Colonel Cargill. Major Major's father, for example, is a rural variant of the same something-out-of-nothing philosophy that worked with such perverse efficiency in big business. Here the business is farming or, more precisely, *not* farming:

> The government paid him well for every bushel of alfalfa he did not grow. The more alfalfa he did not grow, the more money the government gave him, and he spent every penny he didn't earn on new land to increase the amount of alfalfa he did not produce. Major Major's father worked without rest at not growing alfalfa (85).

And the same essential technique, the same tired joke, re-emerges as Heller sets about chronicling the saga of the AmerIndian as emblematically represented in Chief Halfoat's doomed family:

> "Every place we pitched our tent, [Chief Halfoat wails] they sank an oil well. Every time they sank a well, they hit oil. And every time they hit oil, they made us pack up our tent and go someplace else. We were human divining rods. Our whole family had a natural affinity for petroleum deposits, and soon every oil company in the world had technicians chasing us around (44).

As his name suggests, Chief Halfoat is half social commentary, half *schlemiel*; his fate is his bad luck, and his bad luck is his fate. Granted, Heller hardly expects readers to belabor what he presents with the broad strokes of farce. What profit is there in grinding fine what is patently true about American history?

At the same time, however, Heller's sociopolitical agenda is clear, and those who laugh do so knowing full well that they have numbered themselves on the side of the angels. Indeed, in each case Heller's exaggerated portraits drive toward general (and easy) social truths— about the seemingly intelligent who are hopelessly befuddled, about those who turn government subsidies into windfalls, about the continuing exploitation, and stereotyping, of native Americans. Put another way, his platoon on Pianosa may have been served up as a microcosm of a larger American society, but Heller—unlike, say, the Norman Mailer of *The Naked and the Dead*—is more interested in a novel of comic energy than in a novel of Ideas. The result is a version of literary cartooning— one-dimensional portraits designed more with caricature than fully rounded characterization in mind: a Colonel Korn who delivers "corny" speeches to his troops, an Aarfy who is likened to the stylized bark of a friendly dog (in cartoons, invariably rendered as "Awrf, awrf!"), a Major —— de Coverley whose blank represents the enigma he is, and an Orr who will ultimately come to represent an alternative (an "or") to a world divided into the absurdist deaths represented, and justified, by Catch-22 and the survival signified by going AWOL. Moreover, Heller uses the leitmotifs of tag-lines and distinctive clothing to peg his minor characters: Doc Daneeka responds to every crisis by whining, "You think you've got problems? What about me?" while Aarfy is never far from his pipe or McWatt from his red pajamas.

Given the bulk of Heller's novel, repetition figures both as a strategy and at times as a liability. It is, after all, one thing to introduce Major Major's father as a "sober God-fearing man whose idea of a good joke was to lie about his age'' and to repeat virtually the same comic formula with regard to Doc Daneeka (''Doc Daneeka was a very neat, clean man whose idea of a good time was to sulk''). That those reporting to sick call with temperatures below 102 ''had their gums and toes painted with gentian violet solution and were given a laxative to throw away into the bushes'' (33) makes its point better as a single-shot comment than as the running gag it, in fact, becomes. In short, repetition runs rampant in *Catch-22*.

At one point, for example, a character announces that he sees ''everything twice'' and the condition instantly becomes widespread; at another point much the same thing occurs to those with ''flies in their eyes.'' Even the title of the novel—which was originally ''Catch-18,'' but was changed to avoid confusion with the (then) more popular Leon Uris's forthcoming novel, *Mila 18*—seems exactly right for the doubled, and doubling, world it describes. By doubling the number 2, Heller tightens the noose around a world where soldiers ''see everything twice'' and thus throw hospital wards into a panic. But that much said, even an appeal to excess cannot either explain or justify some of the verbal highjinks in *Catch-22*. Given its wide range of wit and self-indulgence (everything from the sophomoric prank to the erudite graduate school allusion), how could it?

Repetition is also at the very heart of whatever structure Heller's chaotic novel might have. The much hinted-at, long-postponed, absolutely crucial confrontation with Snowden (yet another character whose name suggests his fate) may be the book's ''deep image,'' the dark figure in its wacky, comic carpet; but as the freezing ''Snowden of yesteryear'' who perished during the mission over Avignon, the moment of illumination simply won't hold up under some 450 pages of the novel's accumulated weight. "I'm cold . . . I'm cold," Snowden keeps repeating, and finally Yossarian discovers a truth truer than the justifications for war outlined on recruiting posters, truer even than the powerful absurdist grip of Catch-22 itself:

> Yossarian bent forward to peer and saw a strangely colored stain seeping through the coveralls just above the armhole of Snowden's flak suit. . . . [He] ripped open the snaps of Snowden's flak suit and heard himself scream wildly as Snowden's insides slithered down to the floor in a soggy pile and just kept dripping out. A chunk of flak more than three inches big had shot into his other side just underneath the arm and blasted all the way through, drawing whole mottled quarts of Snowden along with it through the gigantic hole in his ribs it made as it blasted out. . . .
>
> He felt goose pimples clacking all over him as he gazed down despondently at the grim secret Snowden had spilled all over the messy floor. It was easy to read the message in his entrails. Man was matter, that was Snowden's secret. Drop him out of a window and he'll fall. Set fire to him and he'll burn. Bury him and he'll rot like other kinds of garbage. The spirit gone, man is garbage. That was Snowden's secret. Ripeness was all (449–50).

Small wonder that Yossarian "circles around" this scene, half suppressing its grisly import, half attracted to its powerful image. But however much he fills in his post-Avignon days by hiding out in the infirmary or by essentially futile gestures of protest (railing at "enemies" out to kill him, moving the bombing line over Bologna, appearing buck naked at a dress parade), he cannot avoid its truth. The point is worth belaboring because some critics have made the coherence, or lack of coherence, in the novel's structure a matter of great import. Most reviewers were content to bathe the novel in adjectives (as one put it, *Catch-22* is a "wild, moving, shocking, hilarious, raging, exhilarating, giant roller-coaster of a book") and leave well enough alone; and most readers were simply overwhelmed by Heller's dazzling verbal *shpritz* (spray)— that is, the rapid-fire piling up of one hilarious episode after another. For such readers the novel was, in a word, *funny*.

However, one measure of the novel's acceptance by the academic community were the painstaking attempts— alas, often contradictory, as it turned out—to demonstrate that the apparent randomness in *Catch-22* was largely an illusion and that the novel had a structure, even a "deep meaning," that its casual readers had missed. In one of the pioneering efforts to find structure where others saw only chaos, Jan Solomon argues that "the most significant aspect of the structure of *Catch-22* is its chronology":

> The major part of the novel, focused on Yossarian, moves forward and back from a pivotal point in time. . . . Yossarian's time is punctuated, if not ordered, by the inexorable increases in the number of missions and by the repetitious returns to the relative safety and sanity of the hospital where "they couldn't dominate Death . . . but they certainly made her behave."
> While the dominant sequence of events shifts back and forth from the present to the past creating any period of time as equally present, equally immediate, a

counter-motion controls the time of the history of Milo Minderbinder. Across the see-saw pattern of events in the rest of the novel Minderbinder moves directly forward from one success to the next.[3]

Solomon's point is that there is a difference between the *illusion* of randomness and mere randomness, between the absurdities a writer consciously creates and those that happen, willy-nilly, in the world. Doug Gaukroger might agree about Heller's art, but in an article seeking to establish *Catch-22*'s structure of time, he argues that Solomon's thesis about mutual, and contradictory, chronologies, simply won't hold up under close inspection. For example,

> If one assumes that Milo's career did not begin until after he first met Yossarian at the time when Colonel Cathcart was demanding 45 missions, then two events (the missing morphine over Avignon, and Snowden's funeral), both of which involve a wealthy Milo in some way, are rendered chronologically impossible because they occur prior to the time of the 45 missions. . . . Excluding the fact that one cannot prove that Yossarian first met Milo at the time of 45 missions (when Yossarian had 38 missions), a large number of other events involve Milo before this time. If only two events were out of time, as has been suggested [in Solomon's article], a case might be made for a dual time scheme; however *all* the events involving Milo occurred at a time prior to the period of 45 missions.[4]

Gaukroger's caveats need to be taken seriously (although perhaps not in the overly earnest way he goes about trying to put the novel into chronological order); nonetheless, there is merit to Solomon's general argument. After all, Yossarian circles around and/or weaves in and out of the crucial scene over Avignon in roughly the same way that Faulkner tells the tale of the rise and fall of Thomas Sutpen's "grand design" in *Absalom, Absalom*. Indeed, Yossarian's zigzagging motions—evidenced in the ways he takes evasive action or engages in fruitless debates at the hospital—identify him like a thumbprint. He means to obliterate the past he experienced over Avignon by living in a continual, and undifferentiated, present tense.

At the same time, however, Gaukroger is clearly right when he argues on behalf of a single chronology, one tied to the number of bombing missions. If Yossarian remains—or perhaps *tries* to remain—static, the number of required missions do not. Therefore, one can establish something like a rough "chronology" of the novel's plot line by paying close attention to the number of missions required before military personnel can be sent home. Generally speaking, the number escalates in integers of fives, and has a nasty habit of being raised just when Yossarian nearly reaches the magic number.

In this sense the bombing missions—whether they be relatively safe "milk runs" or more dangerous affairs— have the look of futile circles (pilots leave their base at Pianosa and return there, thus completing the circle) and cannot help but remind readers of "the soldier in white," the ghoulish study in plaster and gauze, tubes, and interchangeable jars that Yossarian met in the novel's opening pages. What the images share, of course, is a deep sense of futility. In what ways do their meaningless bombing runs differ from the enigmatic soldier in white with a zinc pipe attached to his groin and a feeding tube sewn into the bandages at his elbows? After all, "when the jar on the floor was full, the jar feeding his elbow was empty, and the two were simply switched quickly so that stuff could drip back into him'' (10); and when a flyer nearly reaches the required number of bombing missions, he finds that they have been raised.

By contrast, the tentacles of Milo Minderbinder's ever-expanding empire move in precisely the chronological lines that Solomon suggests. Milo is a study in free enterprise capitalism—with an emphasis on the "free"—and a specialist in the art of the deal. It all begins, as many things do, with an egg. Because Milo Minderbinder controls a vital piece of information—namely, where an enterprising young man can buy an inexhaustible supply of fresh eggs for five cents apiece—and because officers have an equally inexhaustible appetite for fresh eggs, the twenty-seven-year-old wheeler-dealer finds himself earning a barracks promotion to mess officer. Thus is an entrepreneur, and a monster, born. Soon the smell of fresh eggs cooking became virtually indistinguishable from the sweet smell of Milo's success:

> In the beginning General Dreedle devoured all his meals in Milo's mess hall. Then the other three squadrons in Colonel Cathcart's group turned their mess halls over to Milo and gave him an airplane and a pilot each so that he could buy fresh eggs and fresh butter for them too. Milo's planes shuttled back and forth seven days a week as every officer in the four squadrons began devouring fresh eggs in an insatiable orgy of fresh-egg eating. General Dreedle devoured fresh eggs for breakfast, lunch and dinner—between meals he devoured more fresh eggs—until Milo located abundant sources of fresh veal, beef, duck, baby lamb

chops, mushroom caps, broccoli, South African rock
lobster tails, shrimp, hams, puddings, grapes, ice
cream, strawberries and artichokes (140).

To be sure, Milo's flimflamming empire can be written
down in a single word: profiteering. But as Milo might
well insist, what could possibly be more American, more
democratic, than M&M Enterprise, a syndicate in which
everyone owns shares and everyone shares in the profit?
Moreover, isn't capitalism—both as economic system and
individual possibility—what our military forces are fighting to protect? No matter that Milo engineers such outrageous barters that he ends up cornering the market on
Egyptian cotton and tries to fob it off, chocolate-covered,
onto the troops as food, or, worse, that he can work as
easily with the enemy—orchestrating deadly raids that
will presumably "benefit" both sides financially—as he
does with the commodities market. Milo belongs in the
great tradition of amoral Old Southwestern horse traders
that Faulkner drew upon when he had Flem Snopes amble
into Jefferson, Mississippi, looking for opportunity.

Heller, of course, clearly means Milo to be one of
Catch-22's more insidious villains, but he also intends
that he be painted with very different stripes than the
bumbling fools who greedily devour his eggs without a
clue as to how he can buy eggs for seven cents apiece, sell
them for five cents apiece, and still turn a handsome
profit. *That*, as they say, requires a certain amount of perverse genius. But Milo understands the bureaucratic mind
in all its rigidity and lack of imagination—how if the
army has always gotten eggs from Malta, inertia argues
that the army always will. He also understands the advan-
tages of being the "middle man" on both ends of an arrangement, and the ways in which he can take his cut as

buyer *and* seller. Add the happy circumstance of being in a business with virtually no overhead (e.g., an unlimited supply of military aircraft ensures that transportation costs will never upset Milo's delicate apple cart) and the result is a subsidized venture beyond even the wildest dreams of Major Major's father.

At bottom, of course, Milo knows the truth on which all scams depend; namely, that you can't cheat an honest man. In this case, the greed he appeals to is as simple, as innocent, as an egg. Milo simply offers hungry officers the chance to buy eggs at five cents each, and the temptation proves too great to resist. The rest of his empire-building is simply history, a line on a bar graph pointing ever upward.

Solomon's thesis about the crisscrossing chronologies of Yossarian and Milo raises an interesting point, for Yossarian is a man who continually circles past the very lessons that might save him. Milo is such an instructor, albeit one who would argue that greed and survival are inextricably connected. Heller's tone makes it clear that Milo's "patriotism" is the last refuge of the profiteering scoundrel, and that the elaborate mess hall meals ultimately cost wounded fliers the first-aid supplies they badly need. In short, there are no free eggs, much less free lunches.

Given Yossarian's elaborate efforts to find a safe haven, it is curious that he so badly misses the point of Milo's one-man operation. Granted, Yossarian has a playful streak readers admire, and laugh at, but Milo knows how to build job security into what can only be called a risky business. First, he volunteers—yea, even begs—to be given combat duty. As he puts it, "Sir, I want to get in there and fight like the rest of the fellows. That's what I'm here for. I want to win medals, too" (380).

Milo, of course, realizes that Colonel Cathcart just might take him at his word (which, after all, would not be surprising in one as thickheaded, as literal-minded, as Cathcart), but that too is part of Milo's "grand design." Thus, when Colonel Cathcart agrees, and intimates that he'll have Major Major assign him "to the next sixty-four missions so that [he] can have seventy, too," Milo springs his trap. He is only too happy to fly combat missions, but "someone will have to begin running the syndicate for me right away. It's very complicated, and I might get shot down at any time" (380).

The premise thus established, Milo then launches into an "explanation" so entangled, so complicated, so absurd, and of course so funny, that the technique has come to seem Heller's trademark. It begins innocently enough ("Begin with a salt-free diet for General Peckem and a fat-free diet for General Dreedle" (1), but builds by slow integers into a juggernaut of global proportions. Included are deals involving the cedars of Lebanon, peas on the high seas, galvanized zinc and Spanish *naranjas*, and as the last, exasperating straw, the Piltdown Man.

"And—oh, yes. Don't forget Piltdown Man."

"Piltdown Man?"

"Yes, Piltdown Man. The Smithsonian Institution is not in a position at this time to meet our price for a second Piltdown Man, but they are looking forward to the death of a wealthy and beloved donor and . . ." (381).

In a world where individuals are usually characterized as replaceable units, as mere cogs in the Big Machine, Milo has engineered an elaborate, impossibly entangled way of preserving his turf. *Nobody*, the dazed Cathcart soon realizes, could possibly keep all those deals—everything from peas on the high seas to the Piltdown Man—in his head, and nobody but Milo could possibly keep M&M Enterprises afloat. Needless to say, Cathcart is forced to say what Milo has wanted to hear all along; namely, that "you can't fly sixty-four more missions. You can't even fly one more mission" (382). Cathcart is insistent about this, and after all, Cathcart is a colonel. Milo, in short, plays men in much the same way that he manipulates the market—by using the system instead of bucking it, by finding the logical flaw, and saving loophole, in Catch-22's deadly fabric.

By contrast, Yossarian—naked and hiding in a tree after the horror of watching Snowden die—is the very typology of Innocence: Adam and Christ conflated into a single riveting, altogether disturbing image. But while Yossarian may rattle the Colonel Cathcart who lists him among his "black eyes," Yossarian's protests have a "self-evident," commonsensical smack about them that clearly scores points with readers but none with those who live under the shadow of Catch-22. In this sense Yossarian is something of a latter-day Diogenes, desperately searching Pianosa for an honest man.

Meanwhile the casualty list continues to mount, and in increasingly absurdist ways. Some, like Clevinger, fly into a cloud and never return; others are simply "disappeared." And sometimes one grotesque death leads to a chain reaction of deadly absurdities. This is precisely the case when Kid Sampson "leaped clownishly up" to touch the wing of a plane as its pilot playfully buzzed the beach. Suddenly, "something happened"—as Heller will put it ominously in his next novel—and an "arbitrary gust of wind or minor miscalculation of McWatt's senses dropped the speeding plane down just low enough for a propellor to slice him [Kid Sampson] half away.'' At such moments most writers draw the curtain and close off the scene. Heller, however, tends to think of the grotesque as operating on the domino principle, one dark event toppling inevitably into another and another and another. What begins as a landscape rendered in the pastels of innocence (flyers and nurses enjoying a bit of rest-and-recreation at the beach) moves by slow increments to a scene etched in layers of thick black pigment. But, for Yossarian, intimations of mortality were *always* there, even as the others frolicked and the enticing Nurse Duckett did her best to coax him out of his funk and into the company of merrymakers:

> He was haunted and tormented by the vast, boundless ocean. He wondered mournfully, as Nurse Duckett buffed her nails, about all the people who had died under water. There were surely more than a million already. . . . He peered at the vaporous Italian skyline and thought of Orr. Clevinger and Orr. Where had they gone? (347).

And so Yossarian desperately stares at nature, looking for ''signs''—not in quite the way that our Puritan founders understood Providence, but as the brooding, Hamletlike character he is. Nonetheless, Yossarian was prepared for any morbid shock, any manifestation of God's divine, and possibly terrible, plan, except for the darkly comic lesson that McWatt accidently provides.

At eye level what the shocked groundlings see are ''Kid Sampson's two pale, skinny legs, still joined by strings somehow at the bloody truncated hips, standing stock-still on the raft for what seemed a full minute or two before they toppled over backward into the water'' (347); meanwhile, McWatt's plane circles the beach slowly and begins to climb. ''Who's in the plane?'' Yossarian asks, and he soon learns that there are two new pilots on a training flight, along with Doc Daneeka. No matter that Doc Daneeka is on the ground, watching McWatt's plane with the same curiosity as Yossarian and Sergeant Knight, and no matter that Doc Daneeka keeps insisting that ''I'm right here.'' Since he's listed on the flight roster, he is officially in the plane. Meanwhile, McWatt's plane ''kept climbing higher and higher.'' At one point two parachutes pop open (the two new pilots) and thus the scene is set for more grotesque dominos to fall:

''Two more to go,'' said Sergeant Knight. ''McWatt and Doc Daneeka.''

''I'm right here, Sergeant Knight,'' Doc Daneeka told him plaintively. ''I'm not in the plane.''

''Why don't they jump?'' Sergeant Knight asked, pleading aloud to himself. ''Why don't they jump?''

''It doesn't make sense,'' grieved Doc Daneeka, biting his lip. ''It just doesn't make sense.''

But Yossarian understood suddenly why McWatt wouldn't jump, and went running uncontrollably down the whole length of the squadron after McWatt's plane, waving his arms and shouting up at him imploringly to come down, McWatt, come down; but no one seemed to hear, certainly not McWatt, and a great, choking moan tore from Yossarian's throat as McWatt turned again, dipped his wings once in salute, decided oh, well, what the hell, and flew into a mountain (349).

The suicidal gesture kills not only McWatt, but also Doc Daneeka who has absolutely no luck convincing anybody that he is still alive. Since he *must* have been killed in the crash, Doc Daneeka can no longer draw pay or PX rations; he "found himself ostracized in the squadron by men who cursed his memory" (353); and in due time his wife receives the following all-purpose letter from Colonel Cathcart:

> *Dear Mrs., Mr., Miss, or Mr. and Mrs. Daneeka:*
> *Words cannot express the deep personal grief I experienced when your husband, son, father or brother was killed, wounded or reported missing in action* (354).

Mrs. Daneeka, flush with her husband's insurance monies and besieged by suitors, is perhaps the last domino to fall on poor Doc Daneeka. When he writes "begging her to bring his plight to the attention of the War Department and urging her to communicate at once with his group commander, Colonel Cathcart, for assurances that—no matter what else she might have heard—it was indeed he, her husband, Doc Daneeka, who was pleading with her, and not a corpse or some imposter" (354), she is tempted to comply. But Colonel Cathcart's letter (which certainly covers every possible situation—and with "deep personal grief" to boot) clinches the matter: she "moved with her children to Lansing, Michigan, and left no forwarding address." That is how far the grotesque tentacles of a lazy afternoon on Pianosa when "something happened" can eventually reach; and such is the long reach of Death's arm in a novel where bureaucracy is a more efficient killing machine than German bullets.

Yet as horrible as these cascading dominos might be, they pale when compared to Yossarian's ill-fated rescue of Nately's whore's little sister. As a number of critics have pointed out, "The Eternal City" chapter is filled with resonances to Dante's vision of hell, but it is also a contemporary version of the Grail Knight out to rescue innocence from the clutches of a corrupted world. At this point in the novel Yossarian is AWOL, no longer a believer in Catch-22, no longer willing to fly missions (the number has skyrocketed to eighty), and given to "walking backward with his gun on his hip" (413). Moreover, there are ominous signs of a general breakdown back at Pianosa: other flyers are beginning to grumble, and "there was a danger some of them might put on guns and begin walking around backward, too" (414). Attitudes that had formerly belonged to Yossarian alone are becoming widespread. In short, he is no longer the odd man out, the one "crazy" enough to question the authority of Catch-22.

At the same time, however, Yossarian is beginning to move from an interest in mere survival to a position of moral responsibility. Victimhood alone no longer allows one off the hook: "Someone had to do something sometime. Every victim was a culprit, every culprit a victim, and somebody had to stand up sometime to try to break the lousy chain of inherited habit that was imperiling them all" (414). And so, Yossarian's anxious thoughts turn to the young—to the little boys in Africa who "were still stolen away by adult slave traders and sold for money to men who disemboweled them and ate them" (414); to the poor young girls of Rome (a city with its Colosseum reduced to a dilapidated shell and its Arch of Constantine fallen) who have been chased into the mean streets; and especially to Nately's whore's little sister.

But the road from survivor to savior is not an easy one, especially when his increasingly desperate efforts to find the twelve-year-old virgin meet with knowing glances and offers to provide him all manner of young "virgins." Moreover, Rome's streets are swollen with suffering, drowning in cries for help: "The night was filled with horrors, and he thought he knew how Christ must have felt as he walked through the world, like a psychiatrist through a ward full of nuts, like a victim through a prison full of thieves" (424). Even more significantly, the black humor that had both energized and sustained Heller's vision until this point gives way to passages as grim, as stark, as unrelievedly violent as any one can find in contemporary American literature:

> At the next corner a man was beating a small boy brutally in the midst of an immobile crowd of adult spectators who made no effort to intervene. Yossarian recoiled with sickening recognition. He was certain he had witnessed that same horrible scene sometime before. *Dejà vu*? The sinister coincidence shook him and filled him with doubt and dread. It was the same scene he had witnessed a block before, although everything in it seemed quite different. What in the world was happening? . . . The boy was emaciated and needed a haircut. Bright-red blood was streaming from both ears. Yossarian crossed quickly to the other side of the immense avenue to escape the nauseating sight and found himself walking on human teeth lying on the drenched, glistening pavement near splotches of blood kept sticky by the pelting raindrops poking each one like sharp fingernails. Molars and broken incisors lay scattered everywhere (424).

In such a world human life is cheap, as Yossarian discovers when he learns that Aarfy has thrown an Italian girl to her death. Aarfy not only fails to register any remorse, but he argues instead that he really had no choice. After all, he had only raped her *once*, and, as he puts it, "I couldn't very well let her go around saying bad things about us, could I?" (427).

Yossarian is astounded. Not only has he *not* found the girl he's been searching for, but he has arrived too late to protect, to "catch" the Michaela Aarfy tossed out his window like so much garbage. The moment cannot help but remind readers of another would-be protector of innocence, the Holden Caulfield of J. D. Salinger's *The Catcher in the Rye*, as well as Yossarian's meditation over Snowden's flak-riddled body: "Drop him out a window and he'll fall. . . . The spirit gone, man is garbage." The human damage done, all Yossarian can do is insist on justice: "You *killed* a girl," he tells the complacent, pipe-smoking Aarfy. "They're going to put you in jail" (427).

But the brawny MPs who burst through the door aren't after Aarfy. Instead "they arrested Yossarian for being in Rome without a pass" and led him away with a grip "as hard as steel manacles" (429). In a novel filled with contemporary versions of what William Blake once called "mind-forged manacles," there are also moments when physical grips restrain and literal bullets kill. But Heller manages to file even these under the broad general heading of Catch-22.

Like George Orwell's *Animal Farm*—which proves by an impeccable logic all its own that (a) all animals are equal and that (b) some animals are more equal than others, some of the absurdities in *Catch-22* are not only more equal but also more absurd than others. For example, given the bureaucratic noose that systematically tightens around Doc Daneeka's neck, Milo's machinations strike the same absurd tune, but one played in a very different key. After all, the apparent absurdity of buying eggs for seven cents apiece and selling them for five cents apiece is not, strictly speaking, an exercise in absurdity—at least as Heller's novel usually dramatizes the term; rather, it has the simplicity, and the cunning, of genius. In this sense Milo belongs in the same company as Major —— de Coverley, who deflates the cunning and terror of the Glorious Loyalty Oath Crusade with two simple words: "Gimme eat!" Thus, the absurdist reign of Joe McCarthyite machinations—with its reams of meaningless paper and manufactured suspicions—comes to an end.

Yet of all the characters who manipulate the system none is more insidious or more subtle than Orr. He is the one character in *Catch-22* with enough native horse sense and Yankee ingenuity, enough old-fashioned pragmatism, to beat Catch-22 at its own game. He has endless patience, infinite resourcefulness, and best of all quiet confidence. One can hardly imagine two more unlikely roommates: Yossarian rails at an unjust world; Orr stuffs his cheeks with apples. Yossarian, of course, wants justice, while Orr, more modestly, will settle for "apple cheeks." Orr can spend happy hours assembling and disassembling the impossibly tiny parts of a valve so that they will have hot water in the morning.

However, beyond the world of their snug tent Orr is considered a loser, the sort of bad-luck pilot who crashes at the drop or a hat or the dipping of a wing. On one occasion—while Yossarian was still in the hospital after the first disastrous mission over Avignon—Orr's plane had apparently been hit and he "had eased his crippled airplane down gently into the glassy blue swells off Marseilles with such flawless skill that not one member of the six-man crew suffered the slightest bruise." Orr, in short, is a man who has raised the "crash landing" to a high art. Moreover, he apparently welcomes the chance to put the collected wisdom of survival manuals into practice—all the lore about chocolate bars and bouillon cubes, fish hooks, magnetic compasses, and little blue oars the size of a Dixie-cup spoon. Like Orr's tent standard-issue life rafts are jampacked with survival gear, and the infinitely patient, infinitely pragmatic Orr means to take full advantage of the possibilities. As Sergeant Knight describes the scene:

> I swear, you should have seen him sitting up there on the rim of the raft like the captain of a ship while the rest of us just watched him and waited for him to tell us what to do. . . .
>
> Orr began opening up compartments in the raft, and the fun really began. First he found a box of chocolate bars and he passed those around, so we sat there eating salty wet chocolate bars while the waves kept knocking us out of the raft into the water. Next he found some bouillon cubes and aluminum cups and made us some soup. Then he found some tea. . . . Whatever he found he used. He found some shark repellent and he sprinkled it right out into the water. The next thing he finds is a fishing line and dried bait. . . . In no time at all, Orr had that fishing line out into the water, trolling away as happy as a lark. "Lieutenant, what do you expect to catch?" I asked him. "Cod," he told me. And he meant it. And it's a good thing he didn't catch any, because he would have eaten that codfish raw if he had caught any, and would have made us eat it, too, because he had found this little book that said it was all right to eat codfish raw (316–17).

The scene warrants extensive quotation because it so clearly counterpoints Yossarian's epiphanic moment with the dying Snowden. For Yossarian the "truth" that Snowden represents is that man is mutable, that he must die, and this undeniable fact accounts for the death-haunted character of the novel's humor. If Yossarian's rebelliously playful tampering with Washington Irving/Irving Washington invokes the world of the tall tale, his obsession with death reminds us of the clear-sighted protagonist of Mark Twain's *Adventures of Huckleberry Finn*. Huck, of course, ends his tale by having to "light out for the territories" (a land Twain knew full well to be more lawless and brutal than the river towns along the Mississippi) rather than return to "sivilization." As he puts it, he had "been there."

By contrast, just at the moment when Milo and ex-PFC Wintergreen merge (in an image that betokens totalitarian control) and when even Yossarian finally realizes—after allowing Snowden's "secret" to burst full-blown from the unconscious, after his nightmarish and chronologically straightforward account of a journey to the hellish underworld of Rome—that "there is no hope for us, is there?" Heller provides an alternative, an *or*. As it turns out, Orr is alive and well after all. For the chaplain, "It's a miracle, I tell you! A miracle! I believe in God again," (458). After all, what—other than divine intervention—could explain how Orr washed ashore in Sweden after being presumably lost at sea?

Yossarian, of course, knows better. Orr had *planned* his "evasion" to Sweden every bit as consciously, as persistently, as he had set about acquiring "apple cheeks." In a novel where people claim to see things twice, where vision itself is defined either as *jamais vu* (that condition of mind which accepts the strange as familiar) or as *déjà vu* (that condition which accepts the familiar as strange), Yossarian at last has the film on his own eyes stripped away:

> Don't you understand [Yossarian insists]—he planned it that way from the beginning. He even practiced getting shot down. He rehearsed for it on every mission he flew. And I wouldn't go with him! Oh, why wouldn't I listen? He invited me along, and I wouldn't go with him! . . . Now I understand what he was trying to tell me (459).

Armed with the fresh perspective called hope, Yossarian sets off for Sweden. To be sure, he is only inches from the knife of Nately's whore, and at best merely a shaky recruit to Orr's army, but at least he knows that Catch-22 is not invincible, that it can be beaten. After all, who would accuse Orr of going AWOL, of planning the whole thing? Nobody in their right mind "rehearses" crash landings, and nobody imagines rowing—with an implement as ludicrous as a "tiny blue oar"—to Sweden. It is all too absurd, too outlandish—even for the world of Catch-22. But Orr does, and better yet, he did.

Orr banks on the military establishment's general lack of imagination rather like Milo relies on the inertia that always looks to Malta for its egg supply. That is Orr's trump card. Moreover, he has raised the ante of absurdity in ways that go way beyond mere accommodation. For Orr does not merely want to make the best of a bad situation, nor is he especially interested in gestures of protest. Rather, what he wants is the same thing that ostensibly energizes Yossarian—namely, survival.

In a world brimming over with darkly comic deaths Heller's novel moves beyond its broad canvas of biting social satire and grotesque, cartoonish humor to embrace at least the possibility of individual triumph. When others counsel caution or flat out tell him that he won't make it to Sweden, Yossarian answers this way: "I know that. But at least I'll be trying." In *Catch-22* the *trying* is all. Thus, Daniel Walden argues that Yossarian's "desertion to Sweden was an act of faith, an act of opposition to irrationality, a value-goal, an admirable attempt."[5] It is all these, and perhaps more. For Yossarian, like the Ishmael of *Moby-Dick*, is the man escaped to tell the tale—of Kid Sampson and Doc Daneeka, of Colonel Cathcart and General Dreedle, of Milo Minderbinder and ex-PFC Wintergreen, and of the all-important Orr. And Heller has told his tale in ways that forever changed how we think of "war novels" and the comic magic they can spin.

NOTES

1. Heller, *Catch-22* (New York: Simon and Schuster, 1961) 7. Subsequent references are to this edition and are noted parenthetically.

2. Paul Fussell, *Wartime: Understanding and Behavior in the Second World War* (New York: Oxford University Press, 1989) 27.

3. Jan Solomon, "The Structure of Joseph Heller's *Catch-22*," *Critique* (1967): 46–57; rpt. James Nagel, ed. *Critical Essays on Catch-22* (Encino, CA.: Dickenson, 1974) 79.

4. Doug Gaukroger, "Time Structure in *Catch-22*," *Critique*, 12 (1970): 70–85; rpt Nagel: 92.

5. Daniel Walden, "Therefore Choose Life: A Jewish Interpretation of Heller's *Catch-22*" in Nagel: 61.

CHAPTER THREE

Something Happened

In much the same way that Mailer's *The Naked and the Dead* once defined the ambiance of the World War II novel, Sloan Wilson's *The Man in the Gray Flannel Suit* (1955) seemed to capture the angst peculiar to corporate America. To slip between the folds of one's gray flannel suiting and head off from the suburbs toward a public relations job on Madison Avenue was to be the quintessential conformist. As the prevailing arguments would have it, the mass of such men lived twentieth-century versions of what Henry David Thoreau once called "lives of quiet desperation." If William H. Whyte's classic study of corporate life, *The Organization Man* (1956) was Exhibit A, Wilson's best-selling novel was surely Exhibit B. Unfortunately, *The Man in the Gray Flannel Suit* makes for better sociology than it does fiction. What it ultimately sentimentalizes—floating anxieties, vague dissatisfactions, guilt-ridden memories—*Something Happened* renders with a relentlessly chilling candor. The result is an unsparing novel of contemporary manners, one as relentless in its candor as it is meticulous in its accumulation of detail.

Take, for example, what Bob Slocum, the protagonist of Heller's novel, calls "the willies." As he puts it in the novel's opening line, "I get the willies when I see closed doors." No matter that Slocum is a company man doing quite well in his company; no matter that his fears are largely unfounded—Slocum's defining characteristic is dread. "Something" is going to affect him adversely; indeed, so palpable is its ill-defined presence that he can "almost smell the disaster mounting invisibly and flooding out toward me through the frosted glass panes."[1]

Granted, others suffer from assorted floating anxieties, but Slocum's seem a peculiarly advanced case. Again and again his exercise in Kierkegaardian fear and trembling returns to his insistence that "something must have happened to me sometime"—always with the implication that if he could just identify the *something*, he could come to terms with the unsatisfying life that developed afterward. One possibility is that he is a lifelong victim of what Freud calls the "primal scene": "Maybe it was the day I came home unexpectedly with a fever and a sore throat and caught my father in bed with my mother." Or maybe the "something" happened when his father died and Slocum felt guilty and ashamed—not only because he thought he was "the only boy in the whole world who had no father" (1), but also because, by implication, that had been his secret oedipal wish all along.

Heller means to have his psychological cake and eat it, to tease his readers about the figure in Slocum's psychological carpet and to realize that such explanations are too facile by half. Perhaps it is enough to have Slocum admit— and here he speaks for a very large constituency—that

> maybe it was the realization, which came to me early, that I would never have broad shoulders and huge bi-

ceps, or be good enough, tall enough, strong enough, or brave enough to become an All-American football player or champion prizefighter, the sad, discouraging realization that no matter what it was in life I ever tried to do, there would be somebody close by who would be able to do it much better (1–2).

In a word, what Slocum loses early is his *innocence*. Moreover, the quotidian world into which he "falls" is rife with competition, with others who will be bigger, stronger, more aggressive, and more confident. For Slocum this sobering reality describes both the general human condition and his particular fate.

Like *Catch-22*, Heller's second novel was launched by an opening line that simply "came to him"; the bulk of its remaining 500+ pages is given over to elaboration, to embroidery, to efforts at explanation. Slocum cannot make the disparate parts of his life fit, nor can he untangle the mystery of what he calls the *something* that must have happened. The result is a first-person narration filled with fits of paranoia and flights of self-justification. Slocum is a man so totally formed, and so completely deadened, by his environment that categories such as hero or antihero simply do not apply. Rather, Slocum "tells" his story with the flatness of cliché and the predictability of rehearsed response; only Heller's tone, threaded ominously through Slocum's banal descriptions, drives home the point that readers can, and do, also suffer from their own unacknowledged versions of the "willies."

Consider, for example, what Slocum says about curiosity—the urge to *know*—that is the necessary precondition of the tragic persona. In, say, *Oedipus Rex*, piecing together the truth of his story leads to Oedipus' moment of terrible insight. As the argument of tragedy would have it, the hero can never be certain if the knowledge he seeks will save him or destroy him, if it will confirm his suspicions or shatter his illusions. Destiny, however, leaves him little choice. He is fated to know, and to play a prominent part in the unrolling of that fate.

Slocum's tangle of memories has a similar smack of inevitability; he cannot avoid collisions with the painful material that might, just might, explain his present circumstances. Granted, the Slocum who narrates his tale would hardly number himself among those cosy with the tragic spirit. The horrors of contemporary life are so pervasive, so overwhelming, so shivery, that he prefers to make an extended case for ignorance as bliss. As he puts it, "There are so many things I *don't* want to find out," among which are the "kind of games . . . played at the parties my teenaged daughter goes to" (4)—along with the kind of cigarettes they smoke and the pills they swallow—or the precise reason that police cars and ambulances collect down the block. Moreover, Slocum's worries move easily from the local to the general, from specific, identifiable concerns to Worries with a capital W: "And when children drown, choke, or are killed by automobiles or trains, I don't want to know which children they are, because I'm always afraid they might turn out to be mine" (4).

There is a Latin rhetorical figure—*occupatio*—that helps to explain Slocum's technique for keeping, or trying to keep, his obsessions at an arm's length. In roughly the same way that a classical orator might begin a speech by insisting that he will *not* speak about the Roman Empire's might (thereby speaking about it), Slocum mentions—and at some length—what he presumably wishes to avoid.

Occupatio, then, is a means by which one calls attention to something by claiming one will not call attention to it.

In Slocum's case all the roads to *occupatio* lead to the cemetery. As Slocum puts it, in a representative passage as much filled with special pleading as it is with confessional candor,

> I hate funerals—I hate funerals passionately because there is always something morbid about them—and I do my best to avoid going to any (especially my own, ha, ha). At funerals I do have to attend, I try not to speak to anyone; I merely press palms and look overcome. Occasionally, I mumble something inaudible, and I always lower my eyes, the way I see people do in the movies. I don't trust myself to do more. Since I don't know what to say when somebody dies, I'm afraid that anything I do say will be wrong. I really don't trust myself anymore in any tight situation whose outcome I can't control or predict. I'm not even happy changing a fuse or an electric light bulb (5–6).

Slocum's parenthetical asides—which wax ever longer and more insistent as the novel progresses—may strike him as the stuff of wit, but readers are likely to see them as instances of a nervous tic, or as evidence of some deeper desperation. In any event, the very arc of the paragraph—from its initial unease with funerals to its catalog of fear and generalized helplessness—has the effect of inverting the normal rules governing "communication." As Lindsey Tucker puts it:

> Presumably a writer uses parentheses to indicate non-essential information . . . but in reality, information *is* communicated by means of his parenthical phrases and

sentences. Not only do the contents of the parentheses [particularly in later portions of the novel] seem as important as what is said in the remainder of the passage, but often they contradict what is said, and sometimes the parenthetical information has a ring of truth about it that is lacking in the surrounding material. The effect is to reduce information by removing the ordering hierarchies suggested by the parentheses.[2]

Concepts such as information theory and entropy are usually associated with the fiction of Thomas Pynchon, but Tucker makes a convincing case for the part they play in the peculiarities of Heller's style. Communication in *Something Happened* is always on the edge of breaking down, of dissolving, of deconstructing itself into meaninglessness. At one point Slocum observes—parenthetically—that "nothing is suppressed in our family" (240), only to follow with another parenthetical remark that cancels the first one out: "(In our family, everything is suppressed)." Slocum himself is a study in radical contradictions. He is of at least two minds about the possibility of taking over Kagle's job (it is simultaneously meaningless and it matters greatly); about finally being permitted to deliver the three-minute company speech (he *knows* that it will be entirely honorific, yet he desperately wants the "honor"); about his family, his mother, his past, and most of all himself.

In this sense the novel is as much about the failure of speech as it is "about" the genesis of Slocum's pathology or the spiritually deadening effects of contemporary life. Heller, of course, sees these conditions as inextricably (albeit mysteriously) related: Slocum's mother degenerates into silence at one end of the continuum, while his brain-damaged son Derek (significantly enough, the only one of his three children to be graced with a given name) is unable to speak at the other. In between there are office "conversations" artfully designed to communicate intimidation rather than information and domestic chats around the Slocum dinner table that invariably end in shouting matches. Finally, in a novel where manners and mood figure much more prominently than plot, much hangs on whether or not Slocum will be allowed to deliver the convention speech he dutifully prepares each spring. As Slocum observes:

> All my life, it seems, I've been sandwiched between people who will not speak. My mother couldn't speak at the end. My youngest son Derek from the beginning. My sister and I almost never speak. (We exchange greeting cards.) I won't speak to my cousins. (/ may never speak. In dreams I often have trouble speaking. My tongue feels dead and dry and swollen enough to choke my mouth. Its coat is coarse. It will not move when I want it to, and I am in danger and feel terror because I cannot speak or scream.) (332).

The result is the various nervous habits that characterize the "speech" of Slocum's monologue: the verbal tics and unconscious imitations, the catalogs of harangue and the habit of repetition. Consider, for example, this exercise in what Slocum calls "echoing ridicule":

> It's called echolalia.
> It's called echolalia (the uncontrollable and immediate repetition of words spoken by another person. I looked it up. Ha, ha). . . .
> (It can go on forever.)

It can go on forever.
"Shouldn't I be?" I ask.
"Shouldn't you be?" he asks.
"What's up, Jack?"
"What's up, Jack?" (384–85).

Heller is hardly the first postmodernist author to use echolalia as part of a self-conscious effort to throw curve balls at the House of Fiction (in, *Lost in the Funhouse* [1968] John Barth made much of a similar phenomenon called glossolalia), but he is probably the first to raise "mimickry" to such darkly comic heights. Dinners at the Slocum household, for example, are extended exercises in sadomasochism; and while the verbal highjinks may remind readers of the absurdities they first met in *Catch-22*, the effects are both crueler and more familiar than the games aviators such as Yossarian play. "What would you do if I come home with a Black boyfriend?" (130) Slocum's unhappy, fifteen-year-old daughter asks, hoping to bait him into an argument. "I would *still* ask you to clean up your room," Slocum replies, congratulating himself on how nimble, how quick, his answer was. (He then goes on to think to himself: "Of course I'm a racist! And so is she. Who the devil isn't?") The point is that verbal warfare rages both at the office and on the home front, and that while nobody is really *fired* at the company (instead, people get generous "sick leave" benefits, and later even more insurance coverage, and still later are filed away as former employees) and Slocum's domestic situation produces more heartache than catharsis, the very fact that things do not resolve pushes Slocum to search his past for possible explanations. Something *must* have happened to account for the angst-ridden, horrific life he leads in the company and at his "gorgeous two-story wood colonial house with white shutters on a choice country acre in Connecticut off a winding, picturesque asphalt road called Peabody Lane" (334). As the arithmetic of Slocum's "chain of fears" would have it,

> There are five people of whom I am afraid. Each of these five people is afraid of four people (excluding overlaps), for a total of twenty, and each of these twenty people is afraid of six people, making a total of one hundred and twenty people who are feared by at least one person. Each of these one hundred and twenty people is afraid of the other one hundred and nineteen, and all of these one hundred and forty-five people are afraid of the twelve men at the top who helped found and build the company and now own and direct it (9).

In roughly the same way that *Catch-22* sees war as deadly, but not in the usual formula of the "war novel," *Something Happened* regards organizational life as debilitating (indeed, as deadening), but not in the ways that corporations generally conduct business in popular fiction and Hollywood films. Slocum's unnamed company—in which, as he tells his son, he "sells selling"—is a study in benign neglect and organizational inertia—"Salaries are high, vacations are long" (17)—and, as such, its suicide rate (averaging three per year) is simply part of a landscape that includes (and takes into account) heart attacks, cancer, or nervous breakdowns.

Although neither the company's name nor its product is ever revealed, Heller based the initial profile on his years at *Time* magazine, added experiences with *McCall's* (including those as a "presentation writer" who mounted slide and film shows of the sort that Slocum dearly wants to give at his company's annual meeting), and then "stretched" reality into the grotesque shape found in *Something Happened*. As critics have pointed out, in such an organization process becomes more important than product, and status alone provides the satisfaction employees fight for and worry about.

Slocum is one of contemporary literature's consummate worriers. In this sense he is a mirror of the company itself, for it devotes enormous energy to internal analysis—to the making, copying, and distribution of internal reports. Much of the information so assiduously compiled is simply culled from, say, the US Census Bureau (a larger but similar body), and no one in Slocum's company takes such "external reality" very seriously: "People in the Market Research Department are never held to blame for conditions they discover outside the company that place us at a competitive disadvantage. What is, is—and they are not expected to change reality but merely to find it if they can and suggest ingenious ways of disguising it" (28–29). Perceptions of reality are what, in the long run, count. Only fools believe in what they are doing. The rest "come to work, have lunch, and go home. We goose-step in and goose-step out, change our partners and wander all about, sashay around for a pat on the head, and promenade home till we all drop dead" (30).

Slocum worries because his is an ironic self-awareness, one that sees through the sham of what the company defines as success, at the same time remaining blind to any alternatives. Like the speech he dearly wants to give, Slocum realizes that much of what he is supposed to want is meaningless. But that fact alone does not mean he doesn't want it, wouldn't plot to get it, and of course won't worry about the others—those behind closed doors—presumably plotting against him. As Heller once commented, "Slocum has achieved what he has been taught. . . . He wants to be a success," but along the road from formative experiences to adult situations, "something happened" to *satisfaction*. Thus, when he sums up his current status, the result has a look and feel not unlike his matter-of-fact accounts of the company's ironic good fortune. His is a two-car family in a Class A suburb in Connecticut; moreover, "advertising people of the US Census Bureau prepare statistics that include us in the categories of human beings enjoying the richest life" (341).

That Slocum is torn between conformity and rebellion, between wanting to fit in and desiring to break out, marks him as a quintessentially contemporary figure. Indeed, the central thesis of Whyte's *The Organization Man* argues that company directives are never as successful in terms of dictating the small but telling choices of junior executives (i.e., clothing, political affiliations, social clubs, indeed, everything that travels under the large umbrella marked "life style") as an indefinable yet pervasive atmosphere. In short, moments of melodramatic confrontation—the small rule that triggers a showdown at high noon—are to be avoided; rather, companies wear away individuality in roughly the same indetectable way that drops of water reduce a granite cliff. In this sense Heller's novel comes closer than Whyte's study to probing the darker, more insidious aspects of conformity.

For example, a part of Slocum wants to blend into his surroundings so badly that he has become a virtual chameleon, able to take on the tiniest nuances of his environment. Moreover, he does this both compulsively and unconsciously:

> If I am with someone who talks loud and fast and assertively, I will begin talking loud and fast right along with him (but by no means always assertively). If I

am with someone who drawls lazily and is from the South or West, I will drawl lazily too and begin speaking almost as though I were from the South or West, employing authentic regional idioms as though they were part of my own upbringing, and not of someone else's (64).

Woody Allen's *Zelig* is a technically brilliant examination of the same phenomenon: Allen's protagonist can so change his physical demeanor that he is taken for a Chinese laundryman at one point, for a black jazz man at another. On the silver screen the effect is as dazzling as it is funny. To be sure, Allen means to make a seriocomic statement about American-Jewish assimilation (as several of the film's scholarly "witnesses" point out) and to explore those modes of parody that have become his trademark. By contrast, Heller works hard to put as much distance as possible between his gentile protagonist and himself. Ultimately, however, Slocum sees his compulsion to ape the mannerisms of others as a linguistic matter— that is, as one that speaks to writerly, rather than to essentially Jewish, concerns:

> If I talk to a Negro (*spade,* if I've been talking to a honky who calls a spade a spade), I will, if I am not on guard, begin using not only vernacular (militant hip or bucolic Uncle Tom), but his pronunciation. I do the same thing with Puerto Rican cabdrivers; if I talk to cabdrivers at all (I try not to; I can't stand the whining malevolence of New York cabdrivers, except for the Puerto Ricans), it will be on their level rather than mine. (I don't know what *my* level is, ha, ha.) And the same thing happens when I talk to boys and girls of high school and college age; I bridge the generation gap; I copy them: I employ their argot and display an

identification with their tastes and outlooks that I do not always feel. I used to think I was doing it to be charming; now I know I have no choice. (Most of my daughter's friends, particularly her girl friends, like me and look up to me; she doesn't.)

If I'm with Andy Kagle, I limp (66–67).

Slocum, in short, is a plastic man (endlessly flexible, infinitely adaptable) in a plastic world. No hard values give him definition, a norm by which one can judge his actions as heroic or cowardly. Roughly the same thing can be said of the larger world Slocum inhabits; it too is reeling under the throes of entropy as "civilization" itself winds down. Given the correlation, it is hardly surprising that Slocum can move easily—perhaps *too* easily—from his bad feet and deteriorating jawbone to a baleful litany about "summer race riots, drugs, violence, and teen-age sex." Alexander Portnoy, the whining protagonist of Philip Roth's *Portnoy's Complaint,* largely restricts his *kvetching* (complaining) to the cultural forces that make it impossible for him to "enjoy" being bad and that, according to Portnoy's self-serving logic, keep him from becoming a man. In this sense Slocum has a taste for the Bigger Picture: "I've got the decline of American civilization and the guilt and ineptitude of the whole government of the United States to carry around on these poor shoulders" (61–62).

As Slocum argues, only smut and weaponry improve in America; the rest declines in a ceaseless, predictable spiral he calls "downward mobility." But if Slocum can work himself into periodic and highly stylized snits about America's decline, the same is true of Heller himself. Indeed, Heller (who cares about food with a passion not particularly evident in his protagonist) had no difficulty plucking the following passage from *Something Happened* and publishing it separately as an op-ed:

> The world is winding down. You can't get good bread anymore even in good restaurants (you get commercial rolls), and there are fewer good restaurants. Melons don't ripen, grapes are sour. They dump sugar into chocolate candy bars because sugar is cheaper than milk. Butter tastes like the printed paper it's wrapped in. Whipped cream comes in aerosol bombs and isn't whipped and isn't cream. People serve it, people eat it. Two hundred and fifty million educated Americans will go to their graves and never know the difference (453–54).

Where food is concerned, Heller is both a gourmand and a curmudgeon; but in the passage above food is merely a convenient metaphor for all that has gone sour and tasteless. Small wonder that the same people who prefer ''fast'' food (with its imitation ingredients and artificial flavorings) to *real* food are part of the general pattern that might be called the ''crapping up of America.'' Like Slocum, Heller is hardly subtle when it comes to laying on a satiric critique in thick, unrelenting slabs:

> From sea to shining sea the country is filling with slag, shale, and used-up automobile tires. The fruited plain is coated with insecticide and chemical fertilizers. . . . You don't find fish in lakes and rivers anymore. . . . Towns die. Oil spills. Money talks. . . . ''America the Beautiful'' isn't: it was all over the day the first white man set foot on the continent to live (454).

The rub, of course, is that these lines are spoken by Slocum, however much they might reflect Heller's own sensibilities, and Slocum is neither convincing as a character nor reliable as a narrator. Indeed, it is easier—and probably more accurate—to see the junk-riddled landscape as a mirror of Slocum's current state of mind. Dissatisfaction defines his central condition—whether he is worrying his way through a work day, musing about America, or dealing with breakdowns on the domestic front. One telling—and highly visible—by-product of this condition is boredom. Indeed, it would be easy to argue that *Something Happened* revolves around boredom like spokes around a hub, that it is a long and aesthetically risky effort to fill up empty time and space with Slocum's sheer verbosity.

In this sense *Something Happened* is a novel in which one could argue that "nothing" happens. Granted, Yossarian had his innings with the grinding dullness of routine, but he is a rank amateur when matched against a professional time-killer such as Slocum. After all, it is one thing for a Yossarian to subversively "declare war" against various parts of speech (as a censor of enlisted men's letters) and quite another to construct elaborate—and time-consuming—"Happiness Charts." These tables of organization are constructed by "dividing, subdividing, and classifying people in the company on the basis of envy, hope, ambition, frustration, rivalry, hatred, or disappointment" (29). What Slocum discovers is that those who rate the highest are those to whom the company is a job, a place to work, and a temporary one at that. Ask these happy souls if they plan, or even if they would *choose*, to spend an entire life at the company and they would respond with a resounding *No*. By contrast, those clustered at the bottom of the happiness heap are simple-mindedly committed to one goal; namely, to get to the top of the company's organizational ladder.

Slocum falls somewhere in an ill-defined middle: he has no enemies or rivals (that he can think of) and he is "almost convinced" that he can hold his job at the company as long as he wants to. The result puts him in that category of the Happiness Charts reserved for those

> Who are without ambition already and have no hope, although I do want to continue receiving my raise in salary each year, and a good cash bonus at Christmastime, and I do want very much to be allowed to take my place on the rostrum at the next company convention in Puerto Rico (if it will be Puerto Rico again this year), along with the rest of the managers in Green's department and make my three-minute report to the company of the work we have done in my department and the projects we are planning for the year ahead (30).

Modern literature is dominated by characters who cannot reconcile flashes of insight with floods of passion. Among the internal "arguers"—those who move their monologues ever inward by combinations of contradiction, confession, and self-justification—are Dostoevski's testy "underground man," T. S. Eliot's bathetic Prufrock (a man frozen by a fear of social situations, but equally terrified by aloneness), and, of course, Slocum himself. For example, readers are hardly surprised when the "report" Slocum so worries about, and that he finally manages to give—at once fully aware it is inconsequential, yet simultaneously galled by the fact that it is "downright humiliating to be the only one of Green's managers left out"—turns out to be anticlimactic. Indeed, what else could it be, in a novel so wedded to mashing small potatoes into mountains?

Slocum claims that "apathy, boredom, restlessness,

free-floating, amorphous frustration, leisure, discontent at home or at my job—these are my aphrodisiacs now" (385), but an even stronger case can be made on behalf of verbosity. Slocum is reduced to a mouth that tells his story and *tells* it and *tells* it—always from a variety of historical vantage points (rather than perspectives), and always in ways that remain both shadowy and inconclusive. Nonetheless, the story itself—with its effort to unearth the "something" that "happened"—takes on dimensions of its own: justifying, confessional, sexual, indeed everything but the exorcism Slocum hopes it will be.

Time remains the obsession that unifies Slocum's narrative, especially as his reminiscences take on the character of "ghost" stories, of death-haunted chronicles. One need not be a doctrinaire Freudian to agree that doors and gates often function symbolically as indicators of the genital orifice, and that Slocum's paranoia about "closed doors" is related to a series of childhood memories: the darkness of the coalshed where he stumbled over his brother having sex, or the door to the basement storeroom of his first job where an older, more experienced office boy enjoyed regular sex with a secretary. Slocum generally characterizes these moments as lost opportunities that cannot be recaptured, as emblems of life's transience, but they also speak to Slocum's deeper fears about sexuality itself.

At the company Slocum flirts with Jane (an assistant head of the Art Department in Green's department) in ways that "cover the same ground . . . [he] used to exchange with that older girl Virginia under the big Western Union clock in the automobile casualty insurance company." The tableau of a significantly named Virginia, the omnipresent clock under which she sat, and the Kafkaesque insurance company conflates the major themes of *Something Happened* into a single, static emblem. No doubt Heller has intimations of Kafka's experiences at a Prague insurance company in mind as he details the "bank of green metal filing cabinets containing indexes by name to the accident folders filed by number in the taller banks of larger, greener cabinets standing near the front," (70). And no doubt Heller means to suggest how the mind, despite its efforts at repetition and recovery, cannot defeat time. As Slocum sadly admits when his trail of associations leads back to Virginia, whatever might or might not have been, whatever might or might not have happened, "it would have passed, sooner or later just as she has passed already, just as I am passing now" (88). Like the memories of his dead parents, Virginia ends up being "filed away" in Slocum's version of a dead records storehouse. Death, for Heller as well as Slocum, is the ultimate eraser; and what remains—as omnipresent as it is troubling—are

> long gaps . . . that remain obscure and give no clue. There are cryptic rumblings inside them and no flashes of recall. They are pitch black and remain that way, and all the things I [Slocum] was and all the changes and things that happened to me will be lost forever unless I find them. No one else will. Where are they? Where are those scattered, ripped pieces of that fragmented little boy and bewildered young man who turned out to be me? (134)

Slocum's condition—one as idiosyncratic as it is downright bizarre—gradually becomes a scathing, uncompromising portrait of contemporary life. In many respects

Something Happened

Slocum may be monstrous, but he is a familiar monster. Consider, for example, what Slocum says—and more important, how he acts—regarding authority:

> I have this thing about authority, about walking right up to it and looking it squarely in the eye, about speaking right out to it bravely and defiantly, even when I know I am right and safe. (I can never make myself believe I am safe.) I just don't trust it (11).

Slocum is hardly Joseph K, nor is Heller Kafka, but uncertainty and angst, powerlessness and fear, are surely common integers. Slocum retains a lifelong fear that he is about to be fired, although the facts of his life make it clear, first, that he has *never* been fired, and, second, that he *always* receives generous raises and promotions. In short, his is not a Depression-spawned tale on the order of Arthur Miller's *Death of a Salesman* or Saul Bellow's *Seize the Day.* But Slocum can find no way to give the narrative that is his life either a continuous sequencing or a meaning. Indeed, the best answer that Slocum can give to the classical question "Who am I?"—an inquiry that once served as the foundation for Western philosophy and its conception of tragedy—is the following:

> I am a stick: I am a broken waterlogged branch floating with my own crowd in this one nation of ours, indivisible (unfortunately), under God, with liberty and justice for all who are speedy enough to seize them first and hog them away from the rest. Some melting pot. If all of us in this vast, fabulous land of ours could come together and take time to exchange a few words the words would be *Bastard! Wop! Nigger! Whitey! Kike! Spic!* (284–85)

If Slocum's identity is meant to be amorphous, floating, purposefully ill-defined, can the same observations hold true for the novel's title? Apparently *something* happened to create the strange bundle of contradictions known as Robert Slocum, but what? Critics have suggested that no single event—in the traditional novel's sense of "event"—lies in wait for either Slocum or his readers. Rather, what seems to be involved in a shadowy specter that Walker Percy identifies as "some aboriginal disaster, the original sin of the twentieth century." To be sure, Percy's telling remark may reveal more about his own novels than Heller's. A part of Slocum keeps faith with the view that falls from happiness are caused by some primal wrongdoing, but only a part. Other aspects of Slocum's character are far less doctrinaire—and certainly far less consistent—than many readers have imagined.

Great art lies in the details, and herein lies the difference between contemporary novels that throw around general evidence of a protagonist's anxieties, conflicting desires, and ambivalences, and the often excruciating minutiae that *Something Happened* heaps up about these conditions. Heller admits that he initially intended Slocum to be "a fairly loathsome person," but that he was surprised, as the novel progressed, at the amount of sympathy his character was able to command. Granted, much of Slocum's paranoia is simply that—paranoia. Granted too that his obsessive fears are hardly the stuff of which hero-hood is made. Indeed, Slocum alternates between masochistic whining and sadistic cruelty, between a candor that admits a laundry list of faults and behaviors that persistently exemplify them. From the evidence at hand he is an embodiment of what existentialist philosophers call "bad faith."

Something Happened

But, of course, Slocum is more than the sum of his obvious shortcomings. There are also scenes in which one sees not only intimations of a kinder, gentler Slocum, but also the terrible price that such moments exact. For example, consider the moment when Slocum's feelings toward his daughter soften, when he realizes, perhaps for the first time in the novel, that she is also vulnerable:

> I am unable to speak (maybe I do love her), and for a second I am struck with the notion that my wife is right, that perhaps my daughter doesn't hate me and does love me, and perhaps does need to have me know it (and needs to know also, perhaps, that maybe I think well of her). And I begin to feel that maybe *I do care very much whether she hates me or not!* (I don't want her to!) She *must* matter to me, I think, for I am nearly overcome with grief and pity by her look of tearful misery (and I want to cry myself), and I want to put my arms out to her shoulders to hold her gently and console her and confess and apologize (even though I have a vivid premonition suddenly that this is all a typical trick, and she will pull away from me in a taunting, jubilant affront as soon as I do reach out to comfort her, leaving me standing there ridiculously with my empty arms outstretched in the air, abashed and infuriated). I decide to risk it anyway—she is so pathetic and forlorn: I know I can survive the rebuff if it comes. Smiling tenderly, stepping toward her repentently, I reach my hands out to take her in my arms, apologize, and hug her gently.
>
> She pulls away from me with a vicious sneer.
>
> And I find myself standing there stupidly with my empty hands in the air, feeling hurt and foolish (139).

Slocum deserves being quoted at some length, not only to call attention to the troubled heart hidden beneath his thick, distancing armor of mockery and self-laceration, but also to move the focus from the world of work to his equally problematic domestic situation. For example, Slocum not only "wants" a divorce, he *dreams* of divorce, craves a divorce, prays for a divorce. Moreover, he's apparently wanted this divorce all his life: "Even before I was married I wanted a divorce. . . . I was never sure I wanted to get married. But I always knew I wanted a divorce" (484). Behind these stark admissions lies the specter of the dead Virginia Markowitz, who duplicated her own father's death by suicide, and the steamy tale of what she did with others (including a cadre of football players at Duke and presumably the older office boys at the accident insurance company) and what she failed to consummate with the sexually inexperienced Slocum. As his life unrolls, even overcompensation cannot turn the clock back to the Western Union clock under which the fetching, and always eager, Virginia sat. Something happened between that *then* and this *now* which no amount of scathing attack or inner remorse can either explain or exorcise.

Unlike the protagonist of *The Man in the Gray Flannel Suit* (who insists that only his family is "worth a damn"), Slocum's family are alternative versions of himself, ones that "damn" the man he has become. Of the group only his brain-damaged son, Derek, is conspicious by being specifically named; the others—his daughter, his older son, his wife—are anonymous conditions, consistently "flattened out" as characters. The following chapter titles (which also double as their opening sentences) suggest the outlines of the problem each section will fill up with excruciating detail: "My Wife Is Unhappy"; "My Daughter's Unhappy"; "My Little Boy Is Having Difficulties." The last—Slocum's "little boy"— is perhaps the most troubling of all because he becomes a magnet for Slocum's deepest fears and darkest forebodings: "Something terribly tragic is going to happen to my little boy (because I don't want it to)" (364). As Slocum's unbridled fears would have it, his son is the kid who "gets stabbed to death in the park or falls victim to Hodgkin's disease or blastoma of the eyeballs" (321). In short, dark foreshadowings dominate nearly every thought linking father to nine-year-old son. Death runs in Slocum's family (as he characteristically points out), but it is absolutely racing toward their little boy who gives money away to casual friends, feigns illness rather than deliver oral reports, and frustrates his gung-ho gym teacher by refusing to show enough "competitive spirit" in basketball games. As Slocum realizes, "What a nice kid," at the same time he realizes that he is also a doomed one:

> He won't take chances he doesn't have to. (Neither will I. Except with girls, and even then I tend to play it very safe.) He has never, to my knowledge, been in a fist fight. (I wouldn't get in one now either unless it was clearly a matter of life or death. The apple has not fallen far from the tree.) He has no taste for bullying or beating children smaller or weaker. He tries as best he can to avoid associating with anyone he's afraid of, even at the cost of giving up activities he enjoys or forfeiting the companionship of other children he likes (269).

Yet for all his railing, for all his "protests" (many of which are exercises in protesting too much), Slocum is a study in studied resignation—to a wife who has grown older, unexciting, and who drinks far too much; to a daughter who alternately terrifies and annoys him, who knows where Slocum's buttons are and exactly how to push them; to a son whose free-floating anxieties mirror his own; and finally to Derek, the angelic, speechless son he equates with Faulkner's Benjy, the idiot Compson of *The Sound and the Fury.*

Above all else, what Slocum wants to do is survive, although unlike Yossarian he is too sophisticated, too jaded, to believe he has much of a chance. Play by the rules though one might, death is as close as the next phone call (in which he actively imagines hearing that an absurd accident has claimed one of his children) or the suicidal breakdown he tries to ward off by an increasingly desperate humor. Thus, Slocum is the Ordinary writ large—but without the ennobling humanity that might link him with, say, Leopold Bloom of Joyce's *Ulysses.* Rather, his candid account of contemporary *tempora et mores* seems more akin to what John Updike does in his novels of manners about Rabbit Angstrom. For Slocum also sees sexuality as simultaneously attraction and threat, and he is especially undone when it rears its head in the form of a daughter whose open bathrobe covers neither her chest nor her legs:

> I know where my daughter is heading from the girls I know who have already been there. She will not go to church like my wife. . . . She will smoke mari-juana. . . . She will get laid. . . . She will experiment with pep pills (ups), barbituates (downs), mescaline, and LSD, if LSD remains in vogue; she will have group sex (at least once), homosexual sex (at least

once, and at least once with a male present as a spec-
tator and participant), be friendly with fags, poets,
snobs, nihilists, and megalomaniacs, dress like other
girls, have abortions (at least one, or lie and say she
did) . . . I hope she doesn't insist on telling me any of
it (167–68).

And like Rabbit, Slocum comes to the sad realization that
he "cannot fight and nullify a whole culture, an epoch, a
past," (166)—especially when his deepest wish (again,
like Rabbit's) is that when he grows up he wants, above
all else, "to be a little boy," (319).

In short, Slocum spares neither his world nor himself.
He has a habit of speaking to the dark, shameful side of
personality that remains hidden just beneath the level of
articulation. His daughter, by contrast, enjoys father-
baiting nearly as much as Slocum does sadistic teasing.
When she tells him that she wishes she were dead,
Slocum "tells her she will be, sooner or later." When she
tells him that her life is empty and monotonous, he
agrees. When she asks if he had ever thought of killing
himself when he was young, he answers "yes."

By contrast, Slocum's son is too timid, too frightened,
in a word, too *good,* to engage in the Freudian battles that
consume his sister. At nine he is already a veteran sufferer
("frightened," as Slocum puts it, "of just about *everything*") and a good bet to inherit his father's mantle of
victimhood. All he need do is add a few parenthetical
"ha, ha's" and a bit of the Slocum "style." At the
present moment, however, he doesn't strike his combative
sister as quite "real" ("He's never mean. He never gets
mad."), but Slocum knows better. His son is not only no
better off than the rest of them (excepting Derek, the idiot), but, in fact, as his extended aside tries to explain,

([He] may be considerably worse off, in fact, because he is only nine and has already been frightened of just about *everything,* heights and kidnaping, sharks, crabs, drunks, wars, Italians, and me. He isn't afraid of monsters or ghosts so much, because monsters and ghosts are silly. He is afraid of human beings. He veers away from cripples. He welcomes the phenomenon of cops, because he has the dim hope they will safeguard him from all the rest, even from me) (152).

Slocum's heart may crack for such a son—knowing that his innocence is doomed, that his love cannot put their cartoon family back together again—but Slocum is not likely to be confused with a King Lear. The best he can do is banter, and tongue the sore tooth of his regrets:

I believe he pulls us together as a family and keeps us together. (I often think of leaving and always have. My daughter can't wait to get away, or says she can't.) I think we will fall apart as a family when he grows up and moves away. (I love him so much I just know he is going to die.)

"You like him more than me," my daughter has said.

"No," I answer, lying because I do not always wish to outfox her, and because she somehow seems so barren of hope that I find myself grieving silently alongside her, as though at an open coffin or grave in which her future is lying dead already. (She is not yet sweet sixteen, but it sometimes seems to both of us that she has already missed all boats. When?) "But you must admit, darling, that in many ways, he is much more likable."

"I know" (152–53).

And finally, there is Derek, the brain-damaged son that Slocum refuses either to sentimentalize or to falsify. What he reveals (confesses?) is therefore of a piece with his reflections about a wife gone to seed and no longer sexy, about a daughter he actively hates, and a son whose insipid weaknesses (however much masked as "sensitivity") he grieves for. As Slocum insists, it simply isn't true that

> retarded (brain-damaged, idiot, feeble-minded, emotionally disturbed, autistic) children are the necessary favorites of their parents or that they are always uncommonly beautiful and lovable, for Derek, our youngest child, is not especially good-looking, and we do not love him at all. (We would prefer not to think about him. We don't want to talk about him.) (334)

Indeed, the pitiable Derek is akin to Slocum's mother, yet another study in wrecked flesh and speechlessness. And once again, *occupatio*—Slocum's attempt to deny or ignore that which his dismissals merely call attention toward—raises its rhetorical head.

Symmetry brings the angst of *Something Happened* full circle, from its initial emblem of closed office doors and the internecine fears that lie just beneath the company's benevolent exterior to this bitter characterization of Slocum's family:

> In the family in which I live there are four people of whom I am afraid. Three of these four people are afraid of me, and each of these three is also afraid of the other two. Only one member of the family is not afraid of any of the others, and that one is an idiot (333).

Understanding Joseph Heller

Indeed, no word is more charged, more fraught with psychic energy, more repeated, than *fear*. Slocum may "kill time" (apparently the novel's major activity, both in the world of work and in the domestic sphere) by constructing his elaborate Happiness Charts, but he is much more adept at imagining "fear indexes" and in graphing the precise ways that they gain control over lives. And given Slocum's recurrent fantasies about death, it is perhaps not surprising that his darkest dream comes all too true: " 'Something happened!' a youth in his early teens calls excitedly to a friend and goes running ahead." It seems that a crowd has gathered at the shopping center, that a car has gone out of control and mounted the sidewalk, that a plate glass window has been smashed, and that Slocum's little boy is lying on the ground:

> He is screaming in agony and horror, with legs and arms twisted brokenly and streams of blood spurting from holes in his face and head and pouring down over one hand from inside a sleeve. . . . He is panic-stricken. So am I.
> "Daddy!"
> He is dying. A terror, a pallid, pathetic shock more dreadful than any I have ever been able to imagine, has leaped into his face and I can't stand it. He can't stand it. He hugs me. . . . I hug his face deeper into the crook of my shoulder. I hug him tightly with both my arms. I squeeze (524).

As readers learn to their horror, Slocum's son dies of asphyxiation. The other wounds were superficial—lacerations of the scalp and face, a bruised hip, a deep cut on the arm—but nothing that was life-threatening, much less fatal. "Even his spleen was intact." Earlier, when Slocum had tried to embrace his daughter, she had slipped out of his arms and into empty (safe) air; however, when he tries to wrench his son out of time and its relentless kinesis, he succeeds, but only by killing him in the process. Granted, black humor contributes mightily to the casualty lists, and general absurdity, of *Catch-22,* but the telegraphed punch that comes at the end of *Something Happened* suggests an even grimmer note. No doubt those with a predilection for collecting oedipal conflicts will add this one to the heap, duly noting that this is a case in which a son is destroyed by a father, rather than the other way around. And no doubt it would be easy enough to collect the proper supporting evidence for such a view; namely, that in Slocum's professed fears about his son's survival lurks his suppressed desire to turn fear into wish, and wish into *reality.*

A more plausible reading, however, would place greater emphasis on the surd—both in the sense of a sum containing irrational roots and as a voiceless sound—that Slocum has become. He asks but one thing of those who have collected around the death scene: "Don't tell my wife." And with that, Slocum is able to "carry on": moving into Kagle's position, delivering his speech, and removing (at long last) Martha, the crazy typist. Meanwhile, "nobody knows what I've done"—not only in terms of accidently (?) murdering his son, but also in the much broader terms of Slocum's entire life. Something, indeed, *must* have happened to produce such a protagonist—and Heller in effect begins his explanation with the following sentence: "I get the willies when I see closed doors." In an America of nature and wide-open spaces, in an environment conducive to the work ethic and to endless varieties of self-reliance, a Slocum could not have been formed and could not exist. But in a world where the self counts for less than the company, where the social ethic overwhelms traditional standards for moral and immoral behavior (to say nothing of either tragedy or herohood), a Slocum is what one gets. In this sense Sloan Wilson's novel seldom probes beneath his protagonist's gray flannel suit and why he wears it to work. By contrast, *Something Happened* provides something very close to the whole shivery picture.

NOTES

1. Heller, *Something Happened* (New York: Knopf, 1974) 1. Subsequent references are to this edition and are noted parenthetically.

2. Lindsey Tucker, "Entropy and Information Theory in Heller's *Something Happened*," *Contemporary Literature* 25 (1984): 329–30.

CHAPTER FOUR

Good as Gold

Perhaps the first thing to say about Heller's third novel is that, despite the title, it *wasn't*. But for those exasperated by the lack of plot and the confusing chronologies of *Catch-22* and *Something Happened,* at least *Good as Gold* had the look of a conventional novel. It was thick (perhaps overly thick), and it wasn't at all clear how its apparently disparate stories—about the squabbles within a contempory American-Jewish family, about ambitious academic types, about the internecine warfare and plotting among Washington politicos, about bringing down Henry Kissinger—merged into a satisfactory novel; nonetheless, there were whole scenes that struck Heller's fans as pure Heller, complete with the dark, absurdist humor and biting satiric energy that have been his trademarks.

Bruce Gold, the novel's protagonist, bears more than a few resemblances to the unsavory Robert Slocum of *Something Happened.* He is a teacher who hates nearly everything connected with the profession of teaching: his colleagues, his classes, and most of all his students:

> Gold never spent more time on campus than he had to and never went to faculty meetings. He posted a liberal

schedule of office hours but did not keep them. Student conferences were by appointment only, and he never made any. Gold's favorites were those who dropped his courses before the term started. He disliked most the ones whose attendance was regular and whose assignments were completed on time. He was no more interested in their schoolwork than in his own. He arrived in the classroom five minutes late and, to the consternation of all, distributed examination booklets.[1]

Granted, this self-serving regimen gives Gold plenty of time to work on his books. But Gold is as much a charlatan of a scholar as he is a fraud of a teacher: "Gold thought much less of his work than even his fussiest detractors, for he knew far better than they the diverse sources of most of his information and even of much of his language" (44). Of his six published books of nonfiction only the first—an expansion of his doctoral dissertation—was genuine. The rest were increasingly uneven collections of his articles, and "Gold's current scheme for a new collection was a volume of pieces from his previous collections" (44).

Nonetheless, Gold begins the novel with a modest amount of fame under his belt. He is invited to give readings from his work and "had been asked many times to write about the Jewish experience in America" (11). Given his talent and his track record, that is perhaps not unusual (writers are never at a loss for people willing to give them suggestions about where to turn their energies), but in this case Heller's choice of an opening gambit says a good deal about the literary atmosphere in 1979, and about where Heller imagined his own place might be. In short, Bruce Gold was not the only one who had been asked—or who had wondered—if there might be a book in "the Jewish experience in America."

Good as Gold

The rub, of course, is that the American-Jewish literary landscape was already a crowded scene, filled with heavy-hitting competitors such as Bernard Malamud (from whose work Heller takes one of the novel's epigraphs), Saul Bellow, Philip Roth, and countless Sammy-come-lately's and ever-paler carbon copies of the Real Thing. Heller's angle was to come at the subject reflexively, that is, as yet another "project" his protagonist cooks up with an eye squarely fixed on the main chance. As Gold puts it to Lieberman, a friend from the old neighborhood and now the editor of small intellectual magazine, "I would do a sober, responsible, intelligent piece about what it has been like for people like you and me to be born and grow up here. Certainly I'll go at least a little bit into the cross-cultural conflicts between the traditions of our European-born parents and those in the prevailing American environment" (12). No doubt the article he has in mind will be sprinkled generously with terms such as "alienation," "acculturation," and "accommodation"—and it will follow the general contours of Norman Podhoretz's *Making It* (1967). But Gold soon discovers that Lieberman wants something "racier," something with more spice, more *sex*. For him the *real* questions—the ones that generate interest, controversy, and sales—are less concerned with crises of conscience or of faith than they are with "What was it like the first time you saw an uncircumcized cock?" or "How does it feel to be screwing gentile girls?" (13).

The fact that Gold has decidedly limited sexual experience is not important (as far as Lieberman is concerned, he can "fake that part," concentrating on "viewpoints, not facts"); what *is* important is that they settle on a thousand-dollar fee. After all, Lieberman needs an article that will enliven his magazine's deadly dull pages and

Gold needs the money. Out of such mutual interests are publishing decisions made.

In both *Catch-22* and *Something Happened* Heller had taken considerable pains to make his protagonists *non*-Jewish. Arthur Miller had made a similar decision about Willie Loman, the doomed salesman and failed father of his play *The Death of a Salesman*. That is, Miller didn't want to so emphasize Loman's Jewishness that it would detract from the *American* tragedy he was trying to write. Nonetheless, Willie's [Miller's?] speech patterns betray him at every turn, and there are those who continue to see *The Death of a Salesman* as a play very much about the "American-Jewish experience." Roughly the same thing is true for John Yossarian, try as Heller might to give his protagonist a nondescript first name and an "Assyrian" last one. Yossarian, the quintessential outsider, is also—in the minds of many—a distinctively Jewish character. And even Robert Slocum—who lives the corporate life in all its external trappings and interior horror—strikes many as less the creation of, say, a WASP writer John Cheever than somebody one might meet in a novel by an American-Jewish writer such as Bruce Jay Friedman. After all, Slocum himself takes some pains to point out that he looks a bit Jewish to some and that he "thinks Jewish" a good deal of the time.

Thus, Heller may well have realized that his efforts to beat back the rhythms and wisecracks of his Coney Island upbringing were in vain. He may not have given much attention to his Jewishness as a child, as a teen-ager, as a young adult—after all, the "Jewish experience" was all around him, as natural and unconscious as the air one breathed. But its effects, its earmarks, were there nonetheless; they suffused the very posture and gestures he brought to experience. As Gold puts it—in ways that, in most important biographical respects, speak as well for Heller:

> When I grew up in Coney Island, everyone I knew was Jewish. I never realized I was Jewish until I was practically grown up. Or rather, I used to feel that everybody in the world was Jewish, which amounts to the same thing. . . . We had an Irish family on our block with a German surname and there were always a couple of Italians or Scandinavians in my class who had to come to school on Jewish holidays and looked persecuted. I used to feel sorry for them because *they* were the minority (11).

It was time, perhaps, to come clean—and to do it in a novel (*Good as Gold*) which is, at least in part, about how he came to write the book on the ''Jewish experience in America.'' Moreover, to do this Heller would view his protagonist through two very different prisms—first as the ridiculed Jewish son caught in the oedipal grip of a large (and largely assimilated) American-Jewish family, and then as the American-Jewish intellectual caught in slippery folds of governmental doublespeak. In both cases, however, the crossed purposes and missed communications of *Catch-22* are very much in evidence. Here, for example, is how Bruce Gold remembers his first encounter with his stepmother, a meeting that could match the zaniest of Yossarian's run-ins frustration for frustration, absurdity for absurdity, dark comedy for dark comedy.

> Sid had flown to Florida for the wedding and returned with her and his father for a reception at his home in Great Neck. There was an uncomfortable silence after

the introductions when no one seemed sure what to say next. Gold stepped forward with a gallant try at putting everyone at ease.

"And what," he said in his most courtly manner, "would you like us to call you?"

"I would like you to treat me as my own children do," Gussie Gold replied with graciousness equal to his own. "I would like to think of you all as my very own children. Please call me Mother."

"Very well, Mother," Gold agreed. "Welcome to the family."

"I'm not your mother," she snapped.

Gold was the only one who laughed. Perhaps the others had perceived immediately what he had missed. She was insane (27).

Heller's brand of sociology links family life with the dinner table, and it is precisely this equation that Bruce Gold looks upon with dread: his older sisters will exasperate him; his older brother, Sid, will continue his lifelong habit of unfairly one-upping him; he will be positioned at the table so that his knees bang into one of the legs; and no doubt he will, yet once again, find himself the target of his father's tyrannical abuse:

Ashes, Gold grieved wildly, chewing away at his mouthful of mashed potatoes and bread more vigorously than he realized. The food! In my mouth to ashes the food is turning! It has been this way with my father almost all my life.

From the beginning, Gold ruminated now. When I said I was thinking of going into business, he told me to stay in school. When I decided to stay in school, he told me to go into business. "Dope. Why waste time?

It's not what you know. It's who you know." Some father! If I said wet, he'd say dry. When I said dry, he
said wet. If I said black, he said white. If I said white,
he said . . . niggers, they're ruining the neighborhood,
one and all, and that's it. *Fartig* [Yiddish for "fin-
ished"]. That was when he was in real estate. Far
back, that peremptory cry of *Fartig* would instantly
create an obedient silence that everybody in the family
would be in horror of breaking, including Gold's
mother.

It was no secret to anyone that his father considered
Gold a *schmuck*. It would be unfair to say his father
was disappointed in him, for he had always considered
Gold a *schmuck* (33).

Indeed, Julius Gold has a perverse genius for deflating
his son's ego and destroying any vestiges of his self-
confidence. Once when Gold was visiting in Florida,
"his father drew him across a street just to meet some
friends and introduced him by saying, 'This is my son's
brother. The one that never amounted to much.'" And
Alexander Portnoy thought he had complaints! The senior
Gold's *fartig* is every bit as threatening, as castrating as
Sophie Portnoy's overprotective love is smothering. It
signals the end of communication—to any further debate,
discussion, even conversation. Thou shalt not commit
adultery, saith the Lord; Golds do not divorce. *Fartig*.
Thus announceth the latter-day patriarch, Julius Gold.
Writing about *God Knows,* Leon Wieseltier makes the fol-
lowing observations about the techniques and targets of
American-Jewish humor:

America, as is well known, was where Jewish humor
fantastically flourished. It has become perhaps the
most well-known product of American Jewish culture.

But something happened to Jewish humor in America. It shrank in its scope. Its metaphysical commentary, its interest in the collective fate, the dimension of desperation that had made it an essential instrument of the healing heart, all disappeared. As the jokes have gone from Yiddish to English, they have gone from God to parents.[2]

In attempting to explain—and then to dismiss—the humor that undergirds *God Knows,* Wieseltier reveals a good deal more about what is limited, and delimiting, in *Good as Gold.*

There are, of course, not a few ironies in the scorn that Mr. Gold heaps upon his son, and that a serious-minded sort such as Wieseltier might miss. For if the truth be told, Julius Gold is as much the *luftmentsch* (a study in illusion, self-deception, and failure) as he is a Freudian bully. His various businesses include a coat business, a leather business, and assorted ventures in real estate. He was also "in" furs, spices, imports. Most of all, however, he scratched out a meager living—and sometimes not even that—as a tailor. But none of this has dampened Julius Gold's bluster one whit. As he crows at the family dinner table:

Once I owned a store with surgical appliances for people with operations, and I knew how to talk—believe me. I knew what to say to people when it came to selling. "Have I got an arm for you!" I would say to one. "Who sold you that eye?" I would ask another (104).

Generally speaking, Jewish mothers steal the thunder in contemporary American-Jewish fiction. One thinks, for example, of Sophie Portnoy, rather than of her forever constipated husband, as having the most memorably chill-ing lines and the most unforgettable scenes in Philip Roth's novel/indictment of the American-Jewish experi-ence, *Portnoy's Complaint*. But even those who would ar-gue that Jake Portnoy is more than the history of his constipation realize that he is, at best, a minor character in the titanic oedipal conflict that binds Sophie Portnoy forever to her son. By contrast, the volatile Julius Gold not only dominates the domestic landscape (he refuses to eat from chipped china, insisting that such pieces go to his children) but also the world of the old movies as beamed into the living room via television. It is a deftly accurate touch, one that combines Julius Gold's delight in somebody else's obituary with the family's intimations of his mortality:

> Gold's father would move after dinner to the television set in whatever home he had decided to be driven to that evening and begin watching old movies with the energetic vigilance of a custodian of dead souls. The movies themselves made no difference. The responsi-bility for keeping score was only his.
>
> "That one's gone," he would shout elatedly like the grim reaper himself, as though collaring another trophy for his collection. "A hundred years ago. Old age did him in. Remember that lawyer for the defense? *Gesh-torben*. Heart attack. Gone in an instant. Look at that big guy there pushing everyone around. You know where he is today?"
>
> "Dead?" inquired Gold's stepmother delicately, glancing up from her wool. In such moments, she re-called to Gold's mind the image of Madame Defarge knitting at the foot of the guillotine.

"You bet, baby," answered Gold's father. "In *d'rerd*. Now he ain't pushing around people. He's pushing up daisies. A suicide. They tried to hush it up, but they couldn't fool me."

"I do believe," said Gold's stepmother, "that old governess has passed away too."

"Sure, she did," Gold's father agreed. "Cancer. It ate her up. See that taxi driver, the funny one? *Toyt*. Like a doornail. A stroke. Maybe twenty years ago. Lingered a few weeks, then goodbye Charlie. That crooked cop? *Bagruben*. In *D'rerd* also. In a fire, I think. Whiskey had something to do with it too. That one was a *faygeleh* (42).

Julius Gold fears only thing more than death, and that is the word *condominium*. And while there were critics who would make a case for the Golds as emblematic of close-knit Jewish families, the novel will hardly support such sentimental readings. Indeed, *Good as Gold* has more similarities to *King Lear*—especially as the children conspire to unceremoniously dump their father in Miami—than to *Fiddler on the Roof*. As their stepmother Gussie knits away (from an apparently bottomless bag of wool), their father keeps delaying his return to Miami by insisting that he be with the family to observe "the Jewish holidays"—and not merely the High Holidays of Rosh Hashanah and Yom Kippur, but also more minor (and in the Gold family history, obscure) holidays such as Shmini Atzereth (which falls the week before Simchas Torah), Simchas Torah (which celebrates the completion of the year's Torah reading), and Shabbos Bereishes (which begins the Torah reading anew). Here, for example, is what happens at a Gold family dinner—this one

held in a Chinese restaurant amid the wonton soup and
pork spareribs that have become the bill of fare for assimilated American Jews. The trouble starts when Gold
"used the intermission [between ordering pork and its ar-
rival] to utter the unthinkable, the *forbidden:* "What
about your condominium?"

> His father was taken off guard. His jaw dropped and
> his cheeks quivered.
> "Yes," said Sid, joining forces with Gold.
> "Why can't I stay here?" asked Gold's father, and
> added winningly, "I'm no trouble."
> "Pa, I want you to buy that condominium."
> For one moment the old man glanced wildly about in
> hectic disorientation. Blood rushed alarmingly to his
> whole face, and he choked with such anger and violent
> confusion that he seemed to be fighting for each
> mouthful of air. . . .
> "*Vehr Gehargit!*" the old man roared. . . . "I don't
> want no condominium! I live here, not there! It's for a
> vacation I go!"
> Sid was already on his feet, gushing twenty-dollar
> tips and magniloquent apologies like a fountain. Fuck
> him, steamed Gold, dispensing ones and fives with the
> readiest of hollow laughs to dumbfounded children and
> parents at tables nearby. He should be locked up! In a
> prison, not a hospital! In handcuffs! To the walls of a
> dungeon he should be chained, that crazy fuck of a
> bastard, fifteen feet off the ground! (180–81).

And thus scores are kept and evenings with the family
pass. Small wonder that Gold is more interested in making promises, and collecting advances, than he is in doing

research for his study of the American-Jewish experience. Surrounded by his family, Gold finds that his buttons get pushed, that he loses his cool, and, worst of all, that he curses in an ersatz Yiddish not unlike his father's. Could this capacity of sons to duplicate fathers—despite the obvious gains posted by acculturation—end up as a chapter in his book? And what of the loves that may, or may not, be buried beneath his hatreds—for his unappeasable father, for his crazy stepmother, for his conventional sisters and their equally conventional Jewish cooking, for his older brother Sid? Do those possibilities also have to be taken into account? In short, is the shouting, the put-downs, the deflation, the heartburn, and the heartache *all?*

Interestingly enough, Gold's projected book is not *Good as Gold*'s only exercise in hard-cover deception; as Ralph Newsome, Gold's boyhood friend and now something of a Washington insider, admits, the President himself spent his first year in office writing a book about his first year in office. When Gold points out that "most Presidents wait until their terms are over before they write their memoirs," Newsome takes credit for what he sees as a stroke of genius:

> "That was my idea," he admitted. "This way he has a crack at more than just one best seller. He might do one every year. That boosted my stock way up with him too.". . .
>
> "Where did he find the time?"
>
> "We all pitched in and helped," Ralph replied. "Not with the writing, you understand, but with most of the other junk a President has to attend to. . . . Bruce, this President is a very busy man. He has to keep doing so many things a lot faster than he's able

to write about them, even when he's doing nothing more than writing about all the things he's supposed to be doing. That's why he needs all the help he can get'' (49).

As it turns out, Gold had reviewed *My Year in the White House* (praising the President for his willingness to open communications from the start, thus creating a "contemporary universal constituency," and making helpful suggestions about his paragraph organization). The President had liked the review, and now there *seems* to be a job in the offing. Bruce Gold can become one of the President's army of "helpers." The rub, of course, is that Newsome's language is designed to cancel itself out, to zig when one expects a zag, and to zag when one expects a zig. It is, in short, the slippery language of equivocation, endlessly flexible and designed to *almost* say what people desperately want to hear. At one point, for example, Newsome makes it perfectly clear that "we'll want to move ahead with this as speedily as possible, although we'll have to go slowly" (53). At another there is a scene that reads as if it were so much *déjà vu* sliced from *Catch-22:*

"You'll like it here [the White House], won't you? said Ralph, reading his mind.

"Is it always like this?"

"Oh, yes," Ralph assured him. "It's always like this when it's this way."

Gold succeeded in speaking without sarcasm. "How is it when it isn't?"

"Isn't what, Bruce?"

"This way."

"Different."

"In what way, Ralph?"

"In different ways, Bruce, unless they're the same, in which case it's this way."

"Ralph," Gold had to ask, "don't people here laugh or smile when you talk that way?"

"What way, Bruce?"

"You seem to qualify or contradict all your statements."

"Do I?" Ralph considered the matter intently. "Maybe I do seem a bit oxymoronic at times. I think everyone here talks that way. Maybe we're all oxymoronic. One time, though, at a high-level meeting, I did say something everyone thought was funny. "Let's build some death camps," I said. And everyone laughed. I still can't figure out why. I was being serious."

"I think it's time for me to go," said Gold (122).

Oxymorons are, indeed, the linguistic coin of this moronic realm, the language that keeps Gold hoping for 400+ pages. His appointment (possibly as an "unnamed source," and undersecretary, or a cabinet officer) remains precisely that—a possibility among possibilities. What the language of Washington, DC, can nearly "give," it can also hint at taking away. Moreover, if Gold had had precious little experience with anti-Semitism, he finds himself running into its intimations quite regularly in our nation's capital. Early in the game, for example, Ralph Newsome makes it a point to stress that "these are really our golden years," but then adds ominously: "I hope you're making the most of them. A lot of them [fetching

Good as Gold

Washington females] go for your kind." Gold, being Gold, takes up the remark and tries to pin his old school chum down:

> "My kind?" whatever currents of euphoria had been coursing through Gold's veins congealed.
>
> "Yes," said Ralph.
>
> "What do you mean by my kind?" Gold asked Ralph.
>
> "The kind of person you are, Bruce. Why?"
>
> "As opposed to what other kinds, Ralph?"
>
> "The kinds of person you aren't, Bruce. Why do you ask?"
>
> "Oh, never mind," said Gold and then decided to take the inky plunge. "Lieberman thinks you're anti-Semitic."
>
> Ralph was stunned. "Me?" His voice was hurt and astonished. "Bruce, I would feel just awful if I thought I ever did or said a single thing to give you that impression."
>
> Ralph was sincere and Gold was contrite. "You haven't, Ralph. I'm sorry I brought it up."
>
> "Thank you, Bruce." Ralph was placated, and his handsome face fairly shone with grace when he grinned. "Why, I copied your papers at Columbia. You practically put me through graduate school" (121).

Indeed, that Newsome had appropriated Gold's paper on *Tristram Shandy*—and had received a higher grade for it to boot!—is one of the novel's running gags, and yet another piece of evidence (should more be needed) that the race does not necessarily go to either the swift or the bright. Much the same thing is true of Lieberman. In high school Lieberman (always the editor, never the writer) had made life so miserable for Gold that he sent ten of his poems to *The Saturday Review of Literature;* four were accepted. Not to be outdone, Lieberman then submitted twenty-five of *his* poems to the same magazine; thirty-nine came back.

Gold is the darling of such types. Initially people like Lieberman and Pomoroy (a publisher who gives Gold a hefty advance for his projected book on the Jewish experience) need him for the manuscripts he promises; later Newsome and the Washington crowd find Gold a valuable source of catchy, all-purpose phrases. For example, "You're boggling my mind" boggles Newsome's mind: "I'll bet all of us down here can start getting mileage out of that one right away," (51); "I don't know" turns out to be even better, especially when Ron Ziegler, Nixon's press secretary, falls back on it at news briefings:

"Ron, I have to ask you this about the President. Is it that you really don't know or that you don't want to say?"

"I don't know."

"You mean you don't know if you don't know or not?"

"That is correct."

"Thank you, Ron," said the senior correspondent in the first row. "You're to be congratulated. This has been the frankest and most informative press briefing I've ever attended."

"Oh, I don't know" (204).

But the ante *really* goes up when Gold publishes an article entitled "Nothing Succeeds as Planned." Gold's thesis began as an extended meditation on good intentions that invariably go awry, and ended with the conviction that "failure was the only thing that worked predictably," (73). For example,

> The labor movement had come to its end in garbage strikes and gigantic pension funds invested by banks for profit. There seemed no plausible connection between cause and effect, or ends and means. History was a trash bag of random coincidences torn open in a wind. Surely, Watt with his steam engine, Faraday with his electric motor, and Edison with his incandescent light bulb did not have it as their goal to contribute to a fuel shortage someday that would place their countries at the mercy of Arab oil (74).

For the Gold who had once testified in defense of novels by the likes of Henry Miller and William Burroughs and who had once marched with Martin Luther King, Jr., the specter of x-rated films pervading the culture and blacks moving into *his* neighborhood proved deeply upsetting: "To the clear-cut issue of equality had been added the discordant elements of violence, crime, enmity, insurgence, and negation. . . . Things were just not working out as planned" (75).

Gold, of course, alternately worries about and celebrates his new-found neoconservatism, but what he notices most of all is that social chaos is good for business:

> Gold could speak with aplomb now on politics, diplomacy, economics, education, war, sociology, ecology, social psychology, pop psychology, fiction, and

drama—and on any combination of these in infinite permutations, for he had an inventive ability to relate anything to anything else (46).

Moreover, he soon discovered that he could "deliver essentially the same speech to an elderly reactionary religious group that he had given the day before with equal success to a congress of teen-aged Maoists" (46). A talent like Gold's is clearly destined for bigger things, and when the administration begins to realize the potential packed into "Nothing Succeeds as Planned," he is immediately "promoted" from the original post he had not actually been given. After all—as Newsome points out—if every plan is destined to end in failure, the administration is not only justified, but also correct, in doing nothing. In fact, the President himself has a blowup of the proverb on the wall of his breakfast room as "a daily reminder not to attempt to do too much" (117).

The only problem, it seems, is Gold's projected book on the Jewish experience. *That* could cause trouble, and Newsome urges him to "rush that one out while there's still time (119). When an anxious Gold asks, "Time for what?" Newsome coolly replies, "Still time to risk it," (118). Nor is Newsome the only gentile who slyly tweaks Gold about his Jewishness. With Lieberman and Pomoroy quarrels have something of the look and feel of Gold family dinners—that is, the roughened syntax and occasional Yiddish phrasings are the stuff of which a comraderie of sorts is made. By contrast, Pugh Biddle Conover speaks from long and wide experience as a cultural snob and closet bigot. For him, Gold becomes—to his [Gold's] consternation—a variety of Golds: Goldberg, Goldstein, Goldfarb, etc. Only part of the slip can be chalked up to

Good as Gold

senility; his point (namely, Gold's discomfort) is very conscious indeed. Moreover, he is too established, too powerful, too confident to mince his words. The scene begins when Conover offers his increasingly uneasy guest a drink, and then asks that he pour him one as well:

> "I'll have another spot too, if you'll be so good. Oh, a much larger spot than that, Mr. Goldstaub. You pour so sparingly, Mr. Goldsmith, one might think it were your own. You people don't drink much, do you?"
>
> Gold raised his eyebrows. "We people?" A monstrous notion that had been with Gold nearly every day of his adult life was now bulking his thoughts. "What do you mean, sir, by *we people?*"
>
> Conover answered amiably with no loss of equanimity, as though blankly unmindful of any uncomplimentary nuance. "I mean you people don't drink much. There are people who do, Goldstein, and people who don't—"
>
> "Gold, sir."
>
> "—and those who don't, don't, do they? I swear on my life I intended nothing less innocent that that" (p. 236–37).

Later, however, Conover confesses that he finds Gold "pushy," and since Gold (or Goldstein or Goldblatt or whatever) chooses to pursue the matter, he also admits that he doesn't like Jews, and never has:

> Forty or fifty years ago when I had no daughter and still possessed some democratic ideals, I would have championed her marriage to an inferior. Now I'm beyond all prejudice and it's merely a nuisance. A

middle-aged Jew is better than a nigger, I guess, and
not much worse than a wop or a mick. Or somebody
bald! (238)

Like *Catch-22*, this is the stuff that, as Gold's phrase
would have it, "boggles the mind." Even more mind-
boggling, perhaps, is the fact that Gold's own disenchant-
ments with liberal democracy are not as removed from
Conover's obvious prejudices as readers might have supposed. In any event, Newsome dutifully runs neologisms
such as "boggle the mind" past the President and they
invariably receive his enthusiastic seal of approval. Gold,
in a word, has a way with words. But if *Good as Gold* is
filled with echoes from Heller's first novel, it is also re-
plete with reminders of his second. Like the Bob Slocum
of *Something Happened*, Gold must balance apparent success with his even more apparent sense of disappointment.
And in this regard he is hardly alone. His boyhood
chums—Lieberman, the editor of an intellectual quarterly,
and Pomoroy, a publisher—also suffer from the same
floating anxieties and generalized angst:

> For Gold, Lieberman, and Pomoroy, there had been
> sound reason for their expectations. But the real stars
> had sprung from other quarters, and before they knew
> it, they had been left behind. All had gotten what they
> wanted, and felt dissatisfied. Lieberman had wanted to
> edit a small intellectual publication, and he did. Gold
> hoped to obtain a decent teaching post in New York
> and gain some stature as a writer, and he had. Pomoroy
> wanted to be a book editor, and he was. All were suc-
> cessful, and felt like failures (65–66).

Moreover, Gold has reached that moment of truth in which
the gaps between his liberal language and his gut feelings

are beginning to show. If Slocum's candor—about his company, about his domestic situation, about himself—has an unflinching, often monstrous, honesty, the same thing might be said of Gold's exercises in self-relevation:

> And Gold knew something else: he was in a predic-ament, confronted, so to speak, with a crisis of con-science that could not much longer be concealed. All his words had a starkly humanitarian cast; yet he no longer liked people.
>
> He was losing his taste for mankind. There was not much he did like. He liked goods, money, honors. He missed capital punishment, but did not feel he could say so. Gold had a growing list of principles, causes, methods, and ideals in which he no longer believed; and near the top it contained a swelling subdivision of freedoms that included such sacrosanct issues as aca-demic freedom, sexual freedom, and even political freedom. Alternatives were hellish. By no stretch of the imagination could he feel that *this* was what the Founding Fathers had in mind. Either Gold had grown more conservative or civilization had grown progres-sively worse.
>
> Or both (73).

Paul Johnson's recent study, *Intellectuals* (1989), argues that since the French Revolution those intellectuals quick-est to set themselves up as moral authorities and to sug-gest programs for the betterment of mankind have been most prone to feelings of estrangement, even bitterness, toward individual human beings. Moreover, in their zeal for fame and money, Johnson points out, intellectuals from Rousseau onward—for example, Marx, Sartre, Mailer—

often turn out to be scoundrels of the first water. Gold, in a less spectacular way, can be numbered in their camp.

Put another way, dark realities seem to have overtaken Gold's best efforts by way of social criticism, and grave doubts have now replaced his earlier certainties. He still fights against what he sees as his own drift toward neo-conservatism, but he sees the truth of it handwriting everywhere—in the American economic system (''barbarous''), in technology (largely good at mass-producing poverty), in the unrelieved grayness of communism (and this was a revolution that had succeeded).

In this sense, Gold's title—''Nothing Succeeds as Planned''—applies as much to his own ambitions as it does to his social analysis. Like Slocum, Gold is a study in contradiction and self-deception. And he too has learned how to blow with, rather than against, the prevailing winds, to become all things to all people—in short, to blend, chameleon-like, into every woodwork. Thus, ''Gold was a moderate now in just about everything, advocating, in Pomoroy's description, fiery caution and crusading inertia'' (46).

Where Slocum found himself unconsciously aping the speech and physical mannerisms of those around him (with blacks he speaks the lingo either of a militant black or a bucolic Uncle Tom; after an afternoon with Kagle he limps), Gold can adjust his language to the appropriate geography. With his family he affects the characteristic inflections, inversions, and vocabulary of Yiddish (''In my mouth to ashes the food is turning''); in the world of Washington, he learns how to make his sentences double-shuffle with the best of them (''I'm going to work for the government, you see. It's absolutely definite now, although I'm not sure.'') And in academe Gold knows that language is the power by which empires are built:

Good as Gold

Gold prayed also for an endowed chair in the Urban Studies Program that would double his salary while halving his course load. Gold had little doubt he would succeed in Washington if once given the chance, for he was a master at diplomacy and palace intrigue. He was the department's deadliest strategist in the conflict now raging to attract students to subjects in liberal arts from other divisions of the college and to subjects in English from other departments in liberal arts. Gold wrote the most enticing titles and descriptions for the college catalogue, and no one was more successful at originating popular new courses. . . . In the most successful maneuver of all, Comparative Literature had been walled off from texts in translation, while Gold and his English Department were free to pillage the continent at will for such triumphant creations of his as "Dante, Hell, Fire and Faulkner"; "Through Hell and High Water with Hemingway, Hesse, Hume, Hobbes, Hinduism and Others: A Shortcut to India"; "Blake, Spinoza, and Contemporary American Pornography in Film and Literature"; "Sex in World and American Literature"; and "The Role of Women, Blacks, and Drugs in Sex and Religion in World and American Film and Literature." It was now possible, in fact, thanks to the enterprise of Gold, for a student to graduate as an English major after spending all four years of academic study watching foreign motion pictures in a darkened classroom without being exposed for even one moment to any other light but that of a movie projector (138–39).

As Slocum puts it: "I am very good with these techniques of deception although I am not always able anymore to deceive myself (if I were, I would not know that, would I? Ha, ha)." Gold's nervous tics of conscience work a bit differently. When an inner Yiddish voice warns him, *"Zei nisht naarish* [don't be stupid]. Where does somebody like you come off being Secretary of State?" another part of Gold answers brashly: "What's so crazy. . . . It's happened to bigger *schmucks* than me" (124). Nonetheless, both protagonists share the same rest- lessness, and the same capacities for self-delusion. Granted, Slocum *is* the darker, more cynical character, but the Gold who hatches schemes and engineers one publish- ing contract after another is hardly what one would call a naïf. Still, Gold does not see the ways in which his am- bivalences (at once wanting desperately to join Washing- ton's WASP establishment at the same time that he satirically attacks it) signify the larger ambivalences of the "Jewish experience in America."

Nor, one might add, does Heller see the ways in which Gold's obsession with Kissinger—yet another instance of how quirky and unpredictable the Jewish experience in America can become—nearly overtakes, and ruins, the novel. Obviously Heller had been keeping a "file" on Kissinger for some time, and in *Good as Gold* he throws in, verbatim, the most damning press clippings of the bunch—without aesthetic distance or imaginative trans- formation. There is Kissinger on power, on acquiring wealth, on Vietnam, and on the Middle East. Each clip- ping (faithfully reproduced in the novel's text) is followed by a short burst of Gold's scathing commentary. More- over, when Gold rants about Kissinger—*"Zayer klieg* [very smart], that *grubba naar* [vulgar ignoramus], but he was probably making more in undisclosed compensations than Gold earned in salary, even without any under-the- counter *shtupping* [literally, "pushing"] he might still be getting from the Rockefellers" (362)—Gold becomes his father, the very man whose Yiddish tirades and dictatorial certainties so upset him.

As Gold imagines it, the title of his debunking Kissinger book will be *The Little Prussian,* and its thesis would include not only copious examples of Kissinger "Teuton his own horn," but also the charge that he was not Jewish. Gold's father had come to the same conclusion as he watched television footage of Kissinger shuttling back and forth between Israel and the Arab countries. "No Jew was ever a cowboy" (350), the senior Gold declares. *Fartig!* His son, however, plans to finish Kissinger off by beating him at his own game:

> Gold was prepared to develop the thesis that Kissinger was not a Jew in a book of Kissinger "memoirs" he was positive would excite attention and hoped [would] earn him at least a discernible fraction of the *parnusseh* [living] Kissinger was raking in from his own memoirs. . . . Perfect truth was not of determining importance in the exposition of Gold's theory: he felt mutinously that he had as much right to falsehood, bias, and distortion in *his* memoirs of Kissinger as Kissinger did in his own memoirs of Kissinger and had exercised in public office. In Gold's conservative opinion, Kissinger would not be recalled in history as a Bismarck, Metternich, or Castlereagh, but as an odious *shlump* [sad sack] who made war gladly and did not often exude much of that legendary sympathy for weakness and suffering with which Jews regularly were credited (350).

The effect is akin to the white heat and rage that characterizes Robert Coover's portrait of Nixon in *The Public Burning* (1977). Coover, of course, blurs the line between history and fiction in his account of Nixon's role in the execution (the "public burning") of Julius and Ethel Rosenberg, the atomic spies of the 1950s; Heller, by contrast, simply serves up generous helpings of Kissinger's villainry from the daily papers. In both cases, those who agree with the politics are likely to be enchanted by the respective novels; but only the truest of true believers will deny the self-indulgence and sheer overkill that afflict each. Heller's case is a special disappointment because there really *is* a significant novel about the Jewish experience in American hidden within its fatty folds. It is not quite that Gold is, as one character puts it, "a *shonda* [disgrace] to your race," but rather that the postures which worked so brilliantly with the Slocum of *Something Happened* are less effective here.

Good as Gold requires a narrator with richer stuff than Gold's moral/cultural zero can provide. And too, *Good as Gold* is a case of too many talents and too many inclinations galloping off in several directions. In the final pages Heller, grabbing a scene from Chaim Potok's *The Chosen,* watches a group of Coney Island yeshivah boys playing softball. Gold is back on the streets where his long odyssey began. Meanwhile, his brother Sid has died; Andrea Conover (who once loomed, like his Washington appointment, as a possibility just out of reach) has become Ralph Newsome's lover; and his "season in the White House was over." In front of him, however, is a deep image—perhaps the key—to the very book he has been meaning, and unmeaning, to write:

> Athletes in skullcaps? The school was a religious one, a *yeshiva*. Some of the teen-agers had sidelocks, and some of the sidelocks were blond. Gold smiled. God

was right—a stiff-necked, contrary people. *Moisheh Kapoyer,* here it was winter and they were playing baseball, while everyone else played football and basketball.

And a stubborn dispute was in progress. The boy at first base had his back to the others, in a pose of limp exasperation. The pitcher was sulking and refused to throw the ball. The batter was waiting in a squat with his elbows on his knees, his head resting with disinterest on one hand. As Gold watched, the catcher, a muscular, redheaded youth with freckles and sidelocks and a face as Irish or Scottish or Polish as any Gold had ever laid eyes upon, moved wrathfully toward the pitcher with words Gold for a minute had trouble believing.

"*Varf!*" [throw] shouted the catcher. *Varf* it, already! *Varf* the fucking ball!" (447)

Gold picks up his wife at his sister Esther's and returns home. He still owes Pomoroy a book: "Where could he begin?" (447) Two answers strike me as likely: either with "*Varf* the fucking ball!" followed by an analysis that would be pure Gold, or with the novel's opening short paragraph:

> Gold had been asked many times to write about the Jewish experience in America. This was not strictly true. He'd been asked only twice, most recently by a woman in Wilmington, Delaware, where he had gone to read, for a fee, from his essays and books, and, when requested, from his poems and short stories.

The only other possibility is that we have already read the book Gold is at long last prepared to begin. As to which possibility is the correct one, only a Julius Gold is likely to think he knows what it is, and no doubt he would punctuate his pronouncement with a definitive, absolutely final, *Fartig!*

NOTES

1. Heller, *Good as Gold* (New York: Simon and Schuster, 1979) 11. Subsequent references are to this edition and are noted parenthetically.

2. Leon Wieseltier, "Shlock of Recognition," *New Republic* 29 Oct. 1984: 31.

CHAPTER FIVE

God Knows

In *A Connecticut Yankee in King Arthur's Court,* Mark Twain's time-traveling protagonist sits through an interminable performance by Sir Dinadan the Humorist and then observes: "I think I never heard so many old played out jokes strung together in my life. . . . It seemed peculiarly sad to sit here, thirteen hundred years before I was born and listen again to poor, flat, worm-eaten jokes that had given me the dry gripes when I was a boy thirteen hundred years afterwards." But Dinadan's stale fare is as nothing compared with the pranks that Heller's aging King David pulls in *God Knows.* Every Borscht Belt gag, every stage Yiddish cliché, every "bit" from television's Golden Age has been stuffed into King David's 350+ page monologue.

To be sure, the technique of cross-stitching past and present, of introducing contemporary detail into biblical narrative, had been tried before. Nearly thirty years ago Isaac Rosenfeld published a short story entitled "King Solomon" in which the effect worked brilliantly. As his version would have it, Solomon is a demystified, thoroughly domesticated character, one who struck readers as alternately a biblical giant and a contemporary Jewish uncle:

> None [of the counselors] had seen the King's nakedness; yet all have seen him in shirt sleeves or suspenders, paunchy, loose-jowled, in need of a trim. . . . When he appears in this fashion with, say, a cigar in his mouth and circles under his eyes; his armpits showing yellowish and hairy under the arm holes of his undershirt; his wrinkles deep and his skin slack; a wallet protruding from one hip pocket and a kerchief from the other—at such moments, whether he be concerned with issues of government or merely the condition of the plumbing, he does show himself in human nakedness, after all, he is much like any man, he even resembles a policeman on his day off or a small-time gambler. And sometimes, unexpectedly, he summons the cabinet to a game of pinochle.[1]

In *God Knows,* Heller shifts the focus to David, the slayer of Goliath and warrior king, the husband of Bathsheba and father of Solomon, the psalmist *extraordinaire—that* King David. And not surprisingly, Heller's portrait is energized by a similar blurring of then and now, by similar efforts to "humanize" biblical heroes and their legends. At first glance one would not imagine that the author of *Catch-22* or *Something Happened* would be especially drawn to such biblical material; but one of Heller's boyhood friends, George Mandel, recounts how they would read biblical stories and then punch up the narrative lines. Granted, Heller is hardly the first Hebrew school student to have discovered this special, irreverent joy. Then as now wiseacres put their own spin on biblical rhythms: "And He spake. And He spake and He spake a lot to Moses, and then He spake and spake to Moses some more. There was so much spaking it's a wonder Moses had time to walk.''[2]

To be sure, such games are the games of youth, although in Heller's case the inclination survived into adulthood, became ever more elaborate, and finally settled into the making of a novel. Actually, the first indications that Heller was moving in this direction surfaced shortly after he published *Something Happened,* when he toyed with the notion of opening a novel with ''The kid, they say, was born in a manger.'' That notion was quickly abandoned, but one could argue that Heller's attraction to biblical material is part of his long-standing obsession with the vexing issues of authority and justice. For example, the fathers in *Catch-22* (e.g., Nately's, Major Major's) cannot easily separate their own obsessions from their sons. In *God Knows,* Heller takes on the archetypal father and Western culture's embodiment of authority—God.

King David—now at death's very edge—surveys his life and accomplishments, all by way of making a case for his story as the best one in the Bible. After all, David insists,

> Where's the competition? Job? Forget him. Genesis? The cosmology is for kids, an old-wives' tale, a fey fantasy spun by a nodding grandmother already dozing off into satisfied boredom. . . . Where's the action once you get past Isaac and Hagar? Jacob stands up as narrative in a primitive way, and Joseph is pretty lively as the pampered, late-born, bratty favorite of his doting father. But he drops out kind of suddenly as a grown-up, doesn't he? One minute he's dispensing corn and land in Egypt as the pre-eminent agent of the Pharaoh, and just a few paragraphs later he's on his deathbed, breathing his last wish that his bones be car-

ried up from Egypt someday into the land of Canaan. Another headache for Moses, four hundred years later.

Now Moses isn't bad, I have to admit, but he's very, very long, and there's a crying need for variation after the exodus from Egypt. The story goes on and on with all those laws. Who could listen to so many laws, even in forty years? . . . Moses has the Ten Commandments, it's true, but I've got much better lines. I've got the poetry and passion, savage violence and the plain raw civilizing grief of human heartbreak. (5).

Like Slocum of *Something Happened,* King David may be anchored in the physicality of the present—one characterized by a chill that even the luscious Abishag cannot warm, by sexual desires that can no longer be consummated—but his narrative perspective is as free-floating, as associative, as Slocum's. All David's fathers—Jesse, Saul, God—have abandoned him, and in this sense *God Knows* cries out for justice. As he puts it:

Wherever Saul sent me to fight, I went. And the better I was able to serve him in war against the Philistines, the greater grew his envious and furious suspicions that I was slated to replace him and was scheming already to do so. Was that fair? Was it my fault people liked me?

By that time, of course, Saul had been repudiated by Samuel and subjected by God to one of those vast and terrible metaphysical silences that only someone truly almighty and as indispensable as the Lord has the power to inflict. Here I can speak from personal experience: I no longer talk to Him, and He no longer talks to me (7).

Saul is, in short, a study in pathology, a man given to powerful, unpredictable swings of mood—one moment taking David to his bosom, the next plotting to take his life. Indeed, "there were times, it seemed, when he wanted to kill just about everyone, everyone, even his natural son Jonathan." David's monologue is, among other things, an effort to explain, to justify, above all, to *tell* his side of the story. At one point he insists that the *why* behind Saul's murderous rage is simple enough: "I was too good, that's why. (Interestingly enough, Philip Roth's Sophie Portnoy makes an identical claim.) Those were the days when butter wouldn't melt in my mouth." Later, however, David offers a more complicated account of human behavior:

A father-in law [Saul] who spends the better part of his time and strength seeking your death, who sends assassins to your home at night to murder you in the morning and leads armies of thousands of his best soldiers into the wilderness to run you to earth, instead of using them to drive Philistines back down to the coastal plains where they belonged. He offered his daughter to me only in the furtive hope I would be killed collecting the grotesquely low price he set for her. One hundred Philistine foreskins! Saul suffered the paranoid's delusion that even his daughter and his son were in sympathy with me, and he was thoroughly correct. I learned from this a fact applying to everyone that is probably of no practical use to anyone: there is wisdom in madness and strong probability of truth in all accusations, for people are complete, and everybody is capable of everything. There were spooky, tempestuous spells in which killing me was just about the only thing

Saul had on his rabid and demented mind, the poor fucking nut. Go figure him out (7–8).

That David attempts to collect the requisite number of Philistine foreskins by having a group of his men hold down a live Philistine reveals worlds about David's naïveté, his penchant for playing the *schlemiel*. Not only will dead Philistines suffice, but it will also be easier—much easier—to collect the hundred foreskins that Saul requires. And only much later is David able to figure out that Saul is a good deal less interested in a stockpile of Philistine foreskins than he is in finding out that David himself has been killed in the process of collecting them.

In short, David soon regards himself as the undeserving object of Saul's wrath, and that no doubt partially explains why he is so drawn to Jonathan—yet another victim of an autocratic father. But as much as it is true that they become secret sharers, "doubles" each of the other, it is also true that David finds himself irresistibly, fatally, drawn to Saul. In such stories protagonists find themselves returning again and again to a defining moment, to a core event. *Catch-22* is such a story, revolving as it does around Yossarian's memories of Snowden's death on the mission over Avignon; *Something Happened* is such a story, hinged as it is on Slocum's recurring memories of the Virginia who once sat seductively under a Western Union clock; and in no less a fashion *God Knows* keeps returning to David's tragic wish to be reconciled with, and loved by, several father figures. The first, of course, is Saul, the father who unexpectedly withdraws his favor and who seeks instead his death. As David puts it:

I wanted to call him father. I did call him father. Each time I addressed him as my lord the king, I was

calling him father. Each time he answered, he called
me his son. In the years I was near him, I wanted to
hug him. In the years I was distant, I wanted to be
back. . . . He said I would be to him always as one of
his own sons. Had I known at that time how he felt
about his children, this would have been cause for concern (117).

The second surrogate father is the God who kills David
and Bathsheba's child. Saul is written down as a case
study, as a nut only a psychiatrist could understand, but
God is another matter. He is the ultimate enigma, because
of Who He Is, and more importantly, because of What He
Does. That "evil would rise up against me in my own
house" David takes for granted—not because this is the
time-honored maxim of Greek tragedy, but rather because
this turn of events was "taken for granted by every Jewish
parent (18)." But that God should take his child, *that* is
something else, the defining, and dividing, moment.

In this sense, the *kvetching* and wisecracks that so infu-
riated reviewers are so much bluster. Granted, David
means to carve out his rightfully prominent place in literary history by reducing the competition to the stature of
hacks. Moreover, he often does this in ways that seem
nearly as obsessed, as *pathological*, if you will, as Saul's
efforts to destroy David, the "slayer of ten thousands." In
short, they share wide streaks of jealousy and pent-up
rage. What is less clear, however, is if the aged King
David wants his just deserts from posterity or from those
"fathers" who have abandoned and/or punished him.

Take God, for example. There was a time when He and
David "were as friendly as anyone could imagine" (19)—
always sociable, always precise. If David asked God if he

should "go down to Keilah and save the city," God would answer: "Go down to Keilah and save the city." When David asked if he should "go up into Hebron in Judah and allow the elders to crown me king," God replied: "Why not?" What could be easier, simpler, or *nicer*? But looking backward, King David not only realizes that he heard what he wanted to hear, but also that "destiny is a good thing to accept when it's going your way. When it isn't, don't call it destiny; call it injustice, treachery, or simple bad luck" (20).

Heller's King David has the advantage of foresight as well as hindsight. That is, he not only knows what *has* happened but, more important, what *will*:

> Some Promised Land. The honey was there, but the milk we brought in with our goats. To people in California, God gives a magnificent coastline, a movie industry, and Beverly Hills. To us He gives sand. To Cannes He gives a plush film festival. We get the PLO. Our winters are rainy, our summers hot. To people who didn't know how to wind a wristwatch He gives underground oceans of oil. To us He gives hernia, piles, and anti-Semitism. . . . Still, it's the best that's been offered us, and we want to hold on to it (40).

Joab, his adviser, has something of the same gift for farsightedness, but in his case the vision is limited to making a case for pressing their current military advantage. As Joab argues, now that the Israelites have iron (thanks to their victories over the Philistines), "we should strike while it was hot" (259). After all, the English are no longer painting themselves blue, nor are the Germans living any longer in caves. These changes—and others on the horizon—bode ominously for King David's people:

Before you know it, there could be an industrial revolution. Progress can destroy the world. Somebody might discover America. . . . They'll invent democracy and degenerate into capitalism, fascism, and communism. They could find a use for petroleum someday. What would happen if they harness electricity, or invent the internal combustion machine, or the steam engine? You want automobiles? Choo-choo trains? There could be concentration camps. There might even be Nazis. There'll be lots of *goys.* They might not like us. They'll take our religion and forget where it came from (259).

Traditional Jewish humor tends to calculate the costs of "chosenness," and then to ask how it was that the Jews deserved the honor of persecution and pogrom, of humiliation and exile. By contrast, the humor of *God Knows* is cut from the same absurdist cloth as *Catch-22.* Here, for example, is how David imagines Moses talking with God, a situation not unlike Yossarian trying to extract logical sense from *his* superiors:

> "It's a hard life You gave us [Moses points out]."
>
> "Why should it be soft?" spake the Lord.
>
> "And a very tough world."
>
> "Why should it be easy?"
>
> "Why should we love and worship You?"
>
> "I'm God. I AM THAT I AM.". . .

Moses, ever unassuming, was pessimistic about his chances. "Why should they believe me? Why should they follow me? What should I say to them when they ask me Your name?"

> "I AM THAT I AM."

"I AM THAT I AM?"

"I AM THAT I AM."

"You want me to tell them You're I AM THAT I AM?"
(22–23)

Or consider this "bit"—shades of Newsome and Gold
from *Good as Gold*—in which King David declares that
"there is just no way, no way in the world, you can succeed in making Solomon king," only to have Bathsheba
counter with:

> "There is always a way . . . where there is a will."
>
> "Another insufferable platitude from Solomon?"
>
> "That one was mine."
>
> "What does it mean?"
>
> "I don't think I know" (114).

Or this *shtick* as Joab calls King David to task for lisping
when he pronounces the word *pisseth:*

> "Lisping? . . . Who was lisping?"
>
> "You were."
>
> "When?"
>
> "Before."
>
> "Lisping? . . . What are you talking about? I wasn't
> lisping. I never lisp."
>
> "You said pisseth, didn't you?"
>
> "Pisseth?"
>
> "That'th right. You thaid all who pisseth against the
> wall."
>
> "I thaid pisseth? . . . I thaid no thuch thing" (197).

King David's *shtick,* in short, is the sort of stuff that one might hear at a lounge in Jerusalem's King David hotel (e.g., "To the *goyim* He gives bacon, sweet pork, juicy sirloin, and rare prime ribs of beef. To us He gives a pastrami" [24]). It is *kvetching* (complaining) that turns the Bible into "material," that takes its delights in giving contemporary readers the real scoop about, say, Solomon (e.g., "I'll let you in on a secret. . . . He was dead serious when he proposed cutting the baby in half, the *putz*" [12]). What Heller's King David has in common with more contemporary postures is the wisecrack, the flip remark that separates them that's cool from them that ain't. Example: "And a man who lay with a beast, said the Lord, would surely die. And if he doesn't lie with a beast, I would have countered, he won't die?" (28–29) Like virtually all modern humorists, David turns out to be a counter-puncher, one who responds to conventional wisdoms by turning them on their head.

But for all its generous filler of wisecracks and sophomoric humor (e.g., Bathsheba inventing bloomers or Abishag whipping up a round of tacos in the royal kitchen) *God Knows* is more than an endless string of one-liners. The two events that matter centrally to David are the precipitous way God will often withdraw his favor—that, after all, is what occasions Saul's murderous rages—and God's way of punishing fathers by destroying their sons. David realizes full well that an ungrateful child is sharper than a serpent's tooth (after all, he *is* a Jewish parent), and that evil deeds have a way of boomeranging on their doer, but he refuses to believe Samuel's explanation of Saul's behavior at Gilboa—namely, that "it was his destiny" (56). As David sees it, Saul could have waited in the hills and used guerrilla tactics. He could have refused to fight altogether. In short, he could have stopped Samuel's prophecy in its tracks. For David, "character is destiny," which is to say, "Tell us another flood is coming and we'll learn how to live under water" (56). What Samuel calls destiny may be appropriate for Greeks, but not for Jews. Still:

> If character is destiny, the good are damned. In such wisdom is much grief. If I'd known in my youth how I'd feel in old age, I think I might have given the Philistine champion Goliath a very wide berth that day (5).

But slay Goliath David does, and the die, as they say, is cast. If David had known the complications—palace intrigues, civil war, Bathsheba's constant nagging on behalf of Solomon—he would indeed have given Goliath "wide berth." But King David's regrets differ markedly from the "surprises" that so affect gentile heroes from classical tragedy to modern adaptations such as Faulkner's *Absalom, Absalom!* King David *knows* what the protagonists of oedipal formulas painfully discover.

But that God should visit his wrath on David in such relentless, painful ways, and that it should culminate with the slaying of an infant—*that* David hadn't counted on:

> because I had lain with another man's wife, shame of like kind would come to me through mine from a neighbor. That seemed fair enough if it ever occurred. But who could foretell from Nathan's enigmatic words that a son of mine would be the "neighbor" to exact with my wives in the sight of the sun what I had performed with Uriah's wife in shadows and stealth? . . .

I am David, not Oedipus, and I would have broken
destiny to bits. To save my children then, I would have
drawn thunder from the skies. But God, that sneak,
didn't want me to know (18).

David's last remark turns out to be truer than even he had
realized at the time. Thus, when Nathan assures him—as
only a prophet can do—that "the Lord hath lifted the sin
from thee," David thinks: "That was good." And when
he adds, "No harm will come to you," that was even better. But then came, in David's words, the "zinger" and
the cruel "twist":

> "But the child," said Nathan, "shall surely die."
> Trust in the Lord for a twist like that.
> I lost my God and my infant in the same instant
> (19).

Heller's retelling of the biblical tale is indebted to the
version most of us read in the King James translation and,
at the same time, committed to reimagining it in ways that
both humanize David and free him from a long captivity
in talmudic commentary. Indeed, Heller takes the entire
Hebrew Bible as his province. Thus, the story of Joseph,
the pampered, precocious boy with the coat of many colors, and his jealous brothers is duplicated in the life of
David, the harpist. And when David, in desperation,
consults a necromancer to get advice from the spirit of
Moses (after all, didn't Saul himself consult the witch of
Endor on the eve of his fateful battle at Gilboa?), what
he gets instead is Samuel and yet another instance of
crossed communication, of dialogue with a distinctly
Heller touch:

> "I sent for Moses. Don't butt in.". . .

"He's resting. He's still very tired."

"Tell him I have to talk to him. I bet he knows who I am."

"He's deaf as a stone."

"Can't he read lips?"

"He's almost blind now."

"His eye wasn't dim when he died."

"Death sometimes changes people for the worse," said Samuel funereally. "His stutter is back, and bad as ever" (55).

Granted, King David gives his own perspective to events in the King James version (e.g., about Solomon: "If he gives a person the right time, he always asks for it back. He never makes jokes. Do you ever see him laugh?" [103]), but when he settles down—in the middle section of the novel—King David retells the central stories of his life (how he slew Goliath; about Bathsheba and her doomed husband, Uriah; the rape of Tamar and the eventual death of the avenging Absalom; and the chill of old age that even an Abishag cannot warm) with a minimum of embellishment.

Nonetheless, the question still arises: How much does Heller's King David reflect the biblical character of Samuel I and II, and how much of him is simply Heller? The easiest answer, of course, is to say that the King David of *God Knows* is a composite of both, that his sardonic wit and penchant for the absurd has its genesis in the contemporary American author who made such techniques his trademark. On the other hand, however, the impulse to explain, to rationalize, even to justify the questionable behavior of certain biblical characters is part of a much longer tradition. John Friedman and Judith Ruderman argue that it was quite common for a classical rabbi to "explain away" a sin committed by a revered patriarch or sage.[3] Small wonder, then, that the Heller who takes official whitewashings as an invitation to satire should be attracted to a sanitized, and sanctimonious, King David. Heller's midrash (commentary) makes it clear that biblical heroes are thoroughly human beings, but also that they do not require extraordinary efforts by way of explanation; their large ambitions and great deeds are as true—perhaps even truer—when viewed against the backdrop of their human vulnerability. In that light, then, it is a very human David who describes Bathsheba:

> Bathsheba, changing normally with time, is heavier now and shaped with less definition in face and body than when younger. She still proudly has all her front teeth, which are small, crooked and crowded upon each other, and chipped slightly at some of the corners. She was a child, unfortunately, before we Jews took so naturally to orthodontia. It would not matter to me if she lacked some front teeth, for I am in love with Bathsheba and desire her love more than wine, as much as ever before (44).

Again and again the aged King David recalls the image of Bathsheba bathing naked on the rooftop; Bathsheba was his sexual tutor, the one who released him from inhibition and who taught him the language of love both in its physical and linguistic dimensions. For this David, the Song of Songs—from which he quotes liberally—is not the spiritual allegory of God's love for Israel that the rabbis traditionally insisted upon, but an account of physical passion. In rendering Abishag's beauty, David returns to comparisons that have their impetus in echoes from Song of Songs:

> Her figure is flawless, her spirit hypnotic. Her face is as brown garnet, her hair like sable at midnight, her stately neck is a column of molded copper, and her legs from the rear are as pillars of marble set upon sockets of fine gold. Her mouth is most sweet. The scent from between her legs is almost always of apples and acacia, of perfumes out of Lebanon. In front, her navel is like a round goblet that wanteth not liquor, and the patch of her thing is perfectly deltoid and as shiny and indelible as black coral (112).

Language becomes the mode by which David takes possession of the physical, and, more important, language becomes the vehicle whereby David discovers, at long last, that all his life he had wanted love without quite realizing it. In this sense Heller explores the discrepancy between biblical quotation (which he once admitted must certainly be offensive to women) and the more rounded, more humanly interesting, women Heller creates when he allows them to speak.

If there is "irreverence" in *God Knows,* it is less in the highjinks of a Heller juxtaposing the ancient and the contemporary than it is in the Heller who seeks to "correct" God's version of history, to, as it were, turn it into a better story, a superior "fiction." As King David would have it, he is the *victim,* plain and simple. For example, he tries to pass off his culpability in the death of Uriah as Bathsheba's doing, as the "work of the Devil," as a mere response to the prompting of desire, or as a combination of all these things. No matter, the point is that David distances himself from responsibility. Moreover, he is a man beset by scheming wives and a son who gives new meaning to the word *spendthrift:*

> Solomon will bring ruin to us all if he worships strange gods. He'll bankrupt the kingdom with his apes and his ivory and his peacocks. Do you know what he wants for a throne? Here's what he told me he wants for a throne: a great throne of ivory overlaid with best gold, and two carved lions standing by the stays of the throne and twelve more lions—twelve—standing there on one side and on the other upon the six steps (104).

In the "theater" David creates, he casts himself as the man put upon by circumstance, as a man, if you will, more sinned against than sinning. "Is it *my* fault?" he asks repeatedly, and rhetorically.

It is not until relatively late in the novel that David can actually bring himself to call God a murderer, but he has prepared the way by minimizing his own responsibility (repent for *what?* he asks himself) and characterizing God's punishment of Bathsheba's child as an unjust act. For David—as for the other major players of the Bible—the ability to speak directly to God is an indicator of their "specialness," and conversely, God's withdrawal into silence is seen as a sign of God's disfavor. Saul is a textbook case of the latter condition, a man who implodes when God gives him the cold shoulder. On the other hand, Moses—at least as David reanimates his tale—often had the puzzling misfortune of being on the receiving end of information that went from God's lips to his ear. When a baffled Moses asks why God is hardening Pharaoh's heart—only to learn (a) that it will give God an opportunity to show off his powers and (b) that none of this will have made a whit of difference—he protests:

"Then where is the sense?"

"Whoever said I was going to make sense?" answered God. "Show Me where it says I have to make sense. I never promised sense. Sense, he wants yet. I'll give milk, I'll give honey. Not sense" (23).

In David's story as the biblical narrative puts it in II Samuel 12, Nathan plays a prominent part. There David admits his guilt after Nathan delivers the crucial message, prefaced, as always, by the standard formula of prophets—"Thus saith the Lord." Heller's David, however, is not convinced quite so easily. After all, this David is no patsy; besides, only innocents rush in without asking a few pertinent questions first:

"How did He find out?" I wanted to know.

"He has His ways."

"He didn't know where Abel was after Cain killed him, or where Adam hid after they ate the apple."

"Those were trick questions."

"In what language," I asked, "did God address you?" This was a trick question of my own.

"In Yiddish of course," said Nathan. "In what other language would a Jewish God speak?"

Had Nathan said Latin, I would have known he was fabricating (286).

Heller's specialty, of course, is verbal theater—everything from the interplay of disparate languages (the language of the King James Bible, David's earthy Yiddish, Oxford English, even a bit of Gilbert and Sullivan) as David parries with Nathan and the noose of his destiny draws tighter.

Generally speaking, David does not talk with God directly. One instance, however, occurs during an early campaign to unify Israel. Several lines are lifted directly from the biblical account (II Samuel 5)—a practice that Heller would later apply to the Platonic dialogues mercilessly raided in *Picture This*—but with some significant differences in emphasis and interpretation:

> And I inquired of the Lord, "Shall I go up to the Philistines just as I did the time before? Wilt thou deliver them into my hand?"
>
> And the Lord said, "No."
>
> For a moment I was shaken. "No?"
>
> "No."
>
> "What do You mean, no?" I was indignant. "You won't deliver them into my hand?"
>
> And the Lord said, "Do not go up against the Philistines as thou did before."
>
> "What then?"
>
> "But fetch a compass behind them, and come upon them over against the mulberry trees."
>
> "A compass?"
>
> "A compass."
>
> "What's a compass?"
>
> "Encircle them. Ambush them and aggrevate them."
>
> "You're not going to believe this, O Lord," I said, "but I had that same idea myself, of sneaking around them through the mulberry trees on the sides of the plains and pouncing upon them from there and aggravating them from the flanks."

"Sure, sure you did."

"What worries me, O Lord, is the noise we might make as we moved closer to them in the woods and prepare to charge. Is it possible they won't hear us? Wilt Thou deliver them?

"Didn't you already ask Me that?" (252–53)

The result, of course, is that Divinity is diminished, just as biblical heroes have been. But it is also true that the more Heller finds himself grinding through the motions of retelling David's story—however much he might give it a twist here, a Yiddish yank there—the weaker the book becomes. The House of David has fascinated serious writers from William Faulkner (*Absalom, Absalom!*) to Dan Jacobson (*The Rape of Tamar*), but Heller is perhaps the first to take on the whole story—a David's-eye account of how he felled Goliath, the origins and compositional moves that ended with his famous poem to Jonathan, and a detailed history of his loves and lusts—and to render it as if King David were, say, Mel Brooks. Indeed, a good many reviewers pointed out the similarities between *God Knows* and Mel Brooks's hilarious comic monologue entitled "The Two-Thousand-Year-Old Man." That Brooks turns out to be one of Heller's closest friends—and a member of his tightly knit Gourmet Club to boot—only strengthens the identification. But as Heller will detail in his next book—*No Laughing Matter*—much of *God Knows* was written and edited while Heller was suffering a serious siege of Guillain-Barré syndrome, a debilitating breakdown of the nervous system. Brooks, a world-class hypochondriac, was a frequent, and funny, visitor.

However, for all of Heller's wacky, irreverent imagination, the "best lines" in *God Knows* are still to be found in Chronicles, in Judges, and most of all, in I and II Samuel. The notable exception is *God Know*'s last paragraphs, when Heller returns to an aging King David who can no longer be either warmed or sexually aroused by Abishag. He may take careful notice of her powdered arms and legs, her fragrant mouth, but his mind is elsewhere: "I am thinking of God now, and I am thinking of Saul." Moreover, what he sees, as if in a vision, is the image of the eager, bright-eyed boy that was once upon a time himself: "One bare knee of his is bent to the ground, and he is holding in his lap a lyre with eight strings. The apparition has come to play for me." But the music ("soothing, almost divine") is interrupted by an Abishag who approaches "without noise, wearing only a vivid scarf." Kind David's final line says it all—about the alienation and emptiness, the estrangement and odd yearning, that have become his lot: "I want my God back; and they send me a girl."

NOTES

1. Isaac Rosenfeld, "King Solomon," *Alpha and Omega* (New York: Viking, 1956); rpt. Irving Howe, ed., *Jewish American Stories* (New York: Signet Classic, 1977).

2. Heller, *God Knows* (New York: Knopf, 1984) 39. Subsequent references are to this edition and are noted parenthetically.

3. John Friedman and Judith Ruderman, "Joseph Heller and the 'Real' King David," *Judaism* 36 (1987): 300.

CHAPTER SIX

No Laughing Matter

No Laughing Matter—the account of Joseph Heller's bout with Guillain-Barré syndrome (GBS)—has the look of Life imitating Art. Heller suffered his first attack (12 December, 1981) at a time when he was in the middle of writing *God Knows,* a chronicle of, and by, a protagonist who is so weak he can hardly get out of bed. In *No Laughing Matter* a similar condition seemingly traveled to its author, not as an affliction of old age or as just punishment for a sinful life, but unexpectedly, mysteriously, "existentially."

Heller is hardly the first author to have the "surprises" of Art give him or her cause for reflection; but in Heller's case *No Laughing Matter* represented a significant change for the writer whose surrealistic imagination had invented a style as distinctive as his thumbprint. Not only would he be writing about himself—without the aesthetic distancing that fiction represents—but more important, he would be chained to the facts of his medical history. To turn the story of how he was rendered the helpless victim of a sudden and debilitating nervous disorder into a memoir that admirers of *Catch-22* or *Something Happened* could accept was a risky project. Not only would he have to avoid the pitfalls of sentimentality, but also those that come with the territory of "inspirational literature" (e.g., by dint of will power, raw courage, and religious faith, X overcame his or her disability) or what critics of television call "the disease of the week." There were other, more technical problems as well. While it is true that a book such as *No Laughing Matter* would require Heller to write clear paragraphs about increasingly complicated medical procedures, and while it is certainly true that the givens of his situation dictated many of the book's "moves," it would be equally true that *No Laughing Matter* (a cliché of the first water Heller uses for ironic effect) had to somehow be more than a tale of survival. Keeping self-pity and victimhood out (important as that was) could not be sufficient; the real issue would be what Heller had put *in*.

Heller's persona—which, of course, may be a very different matter from the Joseph Heller who one evening found himself physically unable to take off his sweater and who soon found himself in an intensive care unit—is a man ironically blessed with ignorance about the seriousness of his illness or how long it would persist. If jokes about cuckolds depend on everybody except the cuckold being aware of the deceptions swirling around him, Heller's version revolves around those in the know knowing more than he did about the seriousness of GBS. His attending physicians "adopted the sensible approach of not giving me any distressing information about my illness unless they had to," and Heller, for his part, "adopted the sensible defense of not seeking any."[1] All of this is sensible, eminently reasonable, but it is also the stuff of which comic incongruities are made. For example, a longtime friend, the literary critic and biographer Frederick Karl (and a man Heller describes affectionately as walking around with "more factual knowledge in his head than any other human being I know of" [26]), remembers GBS as an adverse by-product of the 1976 national immunization program against swine flu, but conveniently "forgets" to tell Heller that some people really do die from GBS while others remain severely disabled.

Meanwhile, Heller imagines his hospital stay as only an innocent, a naïf, a *schlemiel* can:

> The ingenuous picture I conjured up for myself had me ensconced comfortably on a pile of pillows for hours at a time, reading, writing, dozing, and talking on the telephone—in short, continuing my life in a fashion not much different from what I do in my prime. (24).

The story itself begins as do most of Heller's fictions—that is, in medias res, and with his readers not quite understanding what a letter like the following has to do with Heller:

> In August of 1982 a twenty-six-year-old man in New Jersey wrote to tell me he had been on a respirator in the intensive care unit of a hospital for fifty-eight days and had not been able to talk all that time (7).

Later, of course, we learn that Heller had shared much with the letter-writer from New Jersey; he too had been struck down unexpectedly by GBS. One could argue, of course, that the onset of GBS is usually an occasion for irony, so suddenly and out-of-the-blue does it appear. But in Heller's case the ironies were particularly pointed. He had recently returned to New York City from Aspen, Col-

orado—"lean, bright-eyed, and suntanned" (19). At the
same time, however, the telltale signs of GBS were beginning to make themselves felt. And not surprisingly, Heller
talked about them with his New York friends, never sus-
pecting that the disorder already beginning to tighten its
grip might threaten the capacity for speech itself.

For Heller the ability to talk—to tell stories, to crack
jokes, to one-up friends and antagonists alike—is as necessary, and as natural, as breathing. If *No Laughing Matter* tells the story of Heller's "survival," language is a
large part of the tale:

> Conversation was all that prevented me from going
> mad. I wisecracked boisterously, commented, criti-
> cized, interrupted, counseled. I gave lengthy replies to
> all questions that were asked me by anyone and garru-
> lous responses to thousands that were not. . . . The
> nurses embraced my volubility. To them I was a rarity:
> for all of my twenty-two days in the intensive care unit
> I was usually their only patient who was not com-
> pletely unconscious from one pathological cause or an-
> other. I could hear, I could answer, I could joke, I
> could laugh; and compulsive and insatiable was my ap-
> petite for distraction (8).

A tracheostomy—in which a small incision is made in the
throat so that the GBS sufferer can breathe more effectively—is standard procedure in most cases. Indeed,
Heller's physicians regarded it as "all but inevitable" (8).
The rub, of course, is that Heller would then not have
been able to speak, and as he puts it in retrospect: "I believe now that I would have lost my mind had I not been
able to talk" (8). Indeed, Heller not only talks, but he
talks incessantly—and with a tone, a gruffness, an *edge*

that is only understandable if one understands the ethos of a Brooklyn Jewish childhood. Unlike his friend Speed Vogel, who was inclined to greet every social invitation with an enthusiastic "Yes," Heller's characteristic response to such propositions was a resounding "No!" On the telephone—especially toward strangers—Heller could be nasty, short, even brutish ("What do you want?" was the usual form his impatience took). And Heller's dictum— "A friend in need is no friend of mine!"—was well known among his friends.

Granted, at least half of the bad manners could be chalked up to "style," and those in Heller's circle soon learned both to expect his outbursts and to tolerate them. As Speed Vogel puts it:

> His close and dear friends used to commiserate with each other about his exceptional impatience, rudeness, insensitivity, selfishness, arrogance, duplicity, obstinacy, malevolence, negativity, and general unpleasantness. We liked him . . . but we were extremely hard put to explain why. All of us, in our own ways, tried to apologize to others who happened to meet Heller and whose misfortune it was to be exposed to his charming manifestations. We'd explain that underneath it all he was a good guy. We were less than convincing. People thought we were crazy (13).

The operative word for Heller—one that applies with equal force to everything from his love of words to his voracious appetite for Chinese food—is *more*. His impatience, his gruffness, his lack of sensitivity are merely by-products of larger and, for Heller, more important enthusiasms. And when GBS threatens to bring them to a halt, Heller's chums—including such luminaries as Mel

Brooks, the comic filmmaker and hypochondriac *extraordinaire;* Mario Puzo, author of *The Godfather;* Dustin Hoffman, the actor; and the all-purpose, indefatigable Speed Vogel, whose chapters, and impressions, alternate with Heller's—do their best to bring this antic, excessive spirit inside the hospital's antiseptic walls. Vogel in particular bids for special attention, not only because he virtually dropped his own life to attend to the various details (everything from rounding up pajamas to forging Heller's name on checks) of Heller's incapacitated condition, but also because Vogel creates a persona every bit as cunning, as "literary," as Heller's. As he puts it in *his* opening paragraph:

> I simply can't get *The Picture of Dorian Gray* out of my head. . . . I'm sure it's mere coincidence, but my life started to get terrific at the same exact time that Joseph Heller's got terrible. As he got worse, I got better. As he started to look his age, I started to look more youthful. As he got sicker, I got healthier. As he got poorer, I got to live like a rich man (11).

In short, each becomes the alter ego of the other. At one point early in *No Laughing Matter,* Heller asks Vogel if he would mind moving into his apartment. That way he could take care of the mail, deliver packages, and generally attend to details. As it turns out, Vogel has already moved in—and with some interesting if not altogether "symbolic consequences. As Vogel explains:

> "I thought I might have to go downtown to my studio this afternoon for some winter shirts, but a package from L. L. Bean came to you today with some beauties."

"Is that one of them?" I asked. I had been admiring the corn-flower-blue turtleneck of luxurious texture he had on.

"Do you mind?"

"Of course not," I answered sadly. "But if it looks that good on you, it means I ordered the wrong size for all of them. Where'd you get that trench coat? Is that mine too?"

He looked keenly dashing in the wool-lined trench coat I had purchased at Brooks Brothers just about two weeks earlier and had worn but once. It looked better on him than it had on me (49).

They are also ironic secret sharers with respect to their choice of reading material. Vogel, significantly enough, alludes to *The Portrait of Dorian Gray,* while Heller is associated with copies of Jane Austen's *Emma* and Norman Cousins's *Anatomy of an Illness*—dropped off at Heller's bedside by well-meaning friends unaware that he could not hold them up, much less turn their pages. At first glance *Emma* might seem an odd choice and *Anatomy of an Illness* the more predictable one, but the reverse would be closer to the truth. Heller is hardly a novelist of manners in the Austen mold, but he has a sharp ear for language and a healthy respect for a fellow writer. By contrast, *Anatomy of an Illness* is not only too close to the bone (there is, after all, a case to be made for escapism when one is confined to a hospital bed), but more important, Cousin's account of how laughing at Marx Brothers movies kept up his spirits and in fact warded off a nearly certain medical disaster is precisely the sort of experience—and later, *book*—that Heller is trying mightily to avoid. In this sense *No Laughing Matter* means to be

Heller's tough-minded, and funnier, variation on Cousins's theme. Vogel, on the other hand, is not only propelled into being a ghostly, animate double of Heller, but also into becoming a writer in his own right.

The Heller–Vogel relationship stretched over some twenty-five years, from the time when Speed (so nicknamed by a summer camp counselor in the same ironic spirit that bald men are called Curly) happened to be sitting on a beach reading *Catch-22* and was subsequently introduced to its young author. As the opening line of that novel has it, "It was love at first sight," and somewhat the same thing can be said of the Speed Vogel—Joseph Heller relationship: "I told him I loved it. We became friends. I am not implying that Heller will become an intimate of anyone who likes his work, but it is fair to say that he isn't exactly offended when something he has written is praised" (12).

Nonetheless, Vogel and Heller were, and are, entirely different personality types. Vogel, by his own description, is more than a bit of the *luftmentsch* [literally, "airman"], the sort of person who regards life as a roller coaster. He bounces in and out of a wide variety of jobs (ranging from garment district kingpin to professional herring taster), in and out of money, in and out of various social scenes. By contrast, Heller was, is, and will undoubtedly remain, a *writer.*

At the same time, however, Vogel has a practical side that is utterly missing in the Heller who married when he was twenty-two years old and who, more than thirty years later, still hadn't the foggiest idea how to operate in a laundromat, much less in a kitchen. If pressed, Heller, the bachelor, would not know how to go about scrambling an egg or making a cup of coffee. From Vogel's point of view Heller was not only helpless, but he preferred being that way, so that others would take up the slack. When an appliance broke, Heller simply threw it out and went shopping for a new one. By contrast, Vogel tends to regard a broken appliance as a challenge, and he would set about rounding up screwdrivers and wrenches in an attempt to repair it. As Vogel puts it, probably with less exaggeration than one imagines: "Heller was like someone from another planet" (12). This, in short, is the sort of person who fares badly during a marital separation, and that was precisely Heller's situation when GBS crashed into his already disorganized life.

Enter Speed Vogel, already regarded as the model for one-half of Neil Simon's *Odd Couple,* and now about to launch into a new variation on that theme. Again, it is hard to imagine two more diametrically opposed characters:

> Heller grew up in Coney Island. I grew up in Manhattan. I was a rich kid and was driven to school in our chauffeured limousine. Joe was poor and walked. Later on, when he rode a bicycle, it was for Western Union. I ride one for sport. Joe is tall; I am short (but getting taller). I was a lousy student; Joe was Phi Beta Kappa and a Fulbright Scholar (13).

The pattern that *No Laughing Matter* establishes lies somewhere between point/counterpoint—often with Vogel giving his account of the events surrounding Heller's illness, treatment, and eventual recovery, followed by Heller's confirmations or comic denials; and a plotting, with ironic purposes, of the radically differing arcs that their respective lives took after Heller was stricken. The result is a study in multiple perspectives—the view from inside Heller's skin as balanced, or modified, by the view from outside (Vogel). Modernist literature is especially fond of this strategy (one thinks of Joseph Conrad's *Lord Jim,* F. Scott Fitzgerald's *The Great Gatsby,* or William Faulkner's *Absalom, Absalom!*) as a way of probing beneath consensus reality toward an intimation of the truth. *No Laughing Matter* shares this modernist sense of the truth as uneasily suspended between differing and often complicating viewpoints, but differs on the matter of high seriousness. Repartee, rather than radically isolated consciousnesses, counts for a good deal both in the making and the telling of *No Laughing Matter.* For example, since so much in the book revolves around Heller's legendary appetite and the memorable meals that he consumed in Chinatown with his closest buddies, it is only natural that food should figure prominently when he is forced to receive his nourishment through a nasogastric tube. Such descriptions can be grim stuff, but that is not the case in *No Laughing Matter:*

> I ate, so to speak, from the regular daily menus. Ordering these meals became a ritual of amusement, for everything on the tray was blenderized together in the nurses' section and fed to me through a tube, the process consuming about half an hour. I ordered a lot. I tasted nothing, as I explained to people who asked and heard my answer with looks of incredulity. "Want some?" I would offer generously to anyone present at feeding time. I could go right on talking. I could feel changes in temperature in my throat when anything hot or cold was given me, but nothing else (52).

Evidently Heller's antic spirit was contagious, because on New Year's Eve his nurses offer to pour a glass of champagne down the tube. Heller refused, partly because he was not in the mood for new variations in function or sensation caused by alcohol, and partly because, as he put it, "I never could abide the taste of any but the best champagne" (130). On its most immediate level the repartee between Heller and his visitors, as well as that between Heller and the hospital staff, allows a generous space for wit and even a certain amount of good cheer; but it also suggests something about community, and its necessity for survival.

Heller's troubles began on 12 December, 1981, when he found that he needed Speed Vogel's help to take off a sweater (at the time Heller chalked the bad moment up to static electricity) and when he had trouble eating a sweet potato. As Vogel remembers the fateful evening, "I was taking very little notice of his minor complaints about weakness because he is not very strong and he is inclined to complain. . . . But when he then mentioned that he was experiencing trouble swallowing, I was alarmed" (14).

Although Heller recalls the sweet potato, the rest of Vogel's account is "not exactly the way I remember it." But if some of the individual notes are in dispute, the essential tune is not. When Heller describes his increasing difficulties—he could not cross his right leg over his left; only with difficulty could he raise his left leg at all—to his doctor over the telephone, the response at the other end of the line is immediate: "Guillain-Barré syndrome." At that point Heller knew instinctively that he was headed to the hospital, although he had little idea of the hell awaiting him there. In fact, part of the strategy of *No Laughing Matter* is to split Heller into at least two parts— the one blissfully unaware of what is going on and the other with an obsessive eye on the seriousness of his con-

dition. Here is an example of the first—the naïve—
Heller: "I caught myself planning to pack a variety of
toilet articles and home remedies appropriate to an extended travel adventure" (24).

What this Heller discovers, of course—and what his
"other" renders in excruciatingly realistic, albeit human
(as opposed to clinical) terms—is light years away from
the first description. After a few quick tests—involving
coordination, eye motion, and arm strength—the verdict
is decidedly mixed: on one hand, he is headed to the intensive care unit (ICU); on the other, one of his doctors
assures him that he's probably going to have a mild case
of GBS and that no doubt he will "get everything back"
(29). Significantly enough, the naïve Heller forgets to ask
what he was slated to lose.

In a few short days he discovers just how debilitating
GBS can be. Not only is he unable to hold a book, much
less turn its pages, but even with two thumbs straining he
cannot operate the button on his electric toothbrush. At
the most basic of levels this is indeed "no laughing matter." The contradictions that had been at the center of
Heller's fiction now turn up in dilemmas such as whether
or not to sleep, whether or not perchance to dream:
"What I longed for most in the world was sleep, and
what I began to dread most was getting it":

> Between about four in the afternoon and ten at night, I
> thought I would die from the intensity alone of the fear
> I was suffering in secret as I struggled between a need
> for sleep so enormous it could no longer be staved off
> and a mortal dread of succumbing to it, the petrifying
> foreknowledge that if I drew that one more breath that
> would take me into dreamland, it was going to be my
> last. (121).

As his condition worsens, Heller finds himself fighting first boredom and then deep depression with the darkest humor in his arsenal. Mario Puzo—a man Vogel describes as more willing to "eat a broom," (73) than to make a sick call—was particularly upset by the spectacle of a paralyzed, helpless Heller: "If I was in his spot [he confided to Vogel] . . . I'd rather croak! I'd have to commit suicide!" (73). Unfortunately, Puzo has missed the point—in both its medical and its darkly comic senses. For as Heller points out—calmly and with an indulgent patience—when Vogel passed along his comments: "Ask him how. If you gave me a knife I couldn't use it. I am not able to pull the trigger of a gun. I can't swallow pills. I can't even throw myself out of the window" (73). The blinding quickness and intensity of Heller's response makes Vogel suspicious: how long, he wonders, has Heller been brooding over his options, and systematically watching them evaporate?

But given Heller's retinue of friends, it is hard not to laugh at the spectacle of the assorted do-gooders, well-wishers, and all-around wags who crowd into his hospital room. No doubt Heller did have dark moments when suicide must have crossed his mind, but there must have also been far more moments when he set his mind to coming up with a good gag, a perfectly timed put-down. For example, there is Mel Brooks, a man Heller describes as one of the few people he knew who had ever heard of GBS. But, then again, Brooks "specialized" in knowing about all manner of exotic ailments:

> Standard reference works like the *Merck Manual, Harrison's Principles of Internal Medicine,* and *Dorland's Medical Dictionary* are Mother Goose to him. He is

the only person I'm acquainted with who subscribes to *Lancet,* the English medical journal. As a Boy Scout, his sole merit badge was in first aid (26–27).

This leads to a hilarious bedside visit in which Brooks tries to pass along insider information about Landry's ascending paralysis (a disorder of the peripheral nervous system), while Heller tries just as hard to turn the scene into farce:

> "Mel, Mel," I broke in benevolently when it began to dawn upon me what lay most heavily on his mind. "I know why you're here. I think I can give you what you've come for, the protection you want. I know how to immunize you." I paused to clear my mouth with the suction tube. "I'll have them shave my head and let you rub my baldy for good luck (61).

But Brooks was not amused; when it came to illnesses, he was a serious fellow, and where GBS was concerned, he knew the statistics (one-point-nine per hundred thousand get GBS every year) like his own temperature. Reducing such king-sized anxieties was not going to be easy, but Heller gave it his best shot: "Let me try to build up the odds for you. . . . Not many people have *two* close friends who get it [GBS], right? Can we begin with that?" (61)

And there is Dustin Hoffman, a casual friend for some ten years ("We would get together for dinner or lunch from time to time if we chanced to meet in the same city") who agreed to Heller's curious but eminently pragmatic ground rule: he didn't go to Hoffman's movies, and Hoffman didn't read his books. No doubt both appreciated the other's dry wit:

We greeted each other [in Heller's hospital room] with the sober good humor of a friendly and resigned philosophical ritual.

"You look terrible," was the way I welcomed him. "What the hell has been happening to you?"

"I've been having a rough time," was his straight-faced reply (78).

As the respective narratives of *No Laughing Matter* continue, readers learn, probably to their amazement, that Heller's friends have taken to calling him "the cripple"—partly in the spirit of the gallows humor that Heller's fiction often celebrates, and partly as an elaborate game that represents their version of "grace under pressure." The fact, of course, is that death really did loom just outside the door of Heller's intensive care unit. No doubt Heller began to feel some obligation to keep up the humorous bantering or face the awful prospect of no visitors at all, but nothing in *No Laughing Matter* or in any of the journalism surrounding Heller's bout with GBS suggests that this would have been the case. Heller could have turned dour, depressed, even silent—and his buddies would never have deserted him. And this includes Mario Puzo who, unlike Brooks, has little appetite for hospitals in general or for medical minutiae in particular. As he put it, in what might be one of the best unintentional gags in the book, GBS must be serious stuff indeed because "when they name any disease after two guys, it's got to be terrible" (44). Puzo kept calling to ask if Heller had "croaked" (a favorite Puzo word), but beneath the gangster's idiom and bluster lay genuine concern and unshakable support.

News about the seriousness of Heller's illness leaked to the gossip columns, and soon the general public began to learn the insider news about what had formerly been well-guarded secrets. For example, there was the Gourmet Club, a social phenomenon that in its own way rivals the rituals and highjinks observed around the Algonquin Hotel's famous "round table" by the likes of Dorothy Parker, Robert Benchley, and other wits from *The New Yorker* magazine and the Broadway stage. Heller describes the Gourmet Club, an all-male group dedicated to scouring Chinatown for the best restaurants, eating huge amounts of food, and then searching old haunts in Brooklyn for the perfect egg cream (a drink made from milk, seltzer, and chocolate syrup) as if it were the Holy Grail:

> All of those lousy bastards were going out to dinner in Chinatown without me. . . . Speed, George, Julie Green, Joe Stein expressed sincere and sorrowful regret at leaving me there while they went down to Chinatown. Who could believe them? Those liars, those hypocrites! They looked so eager (94–95).

Among *No Laughing Matter*'s strategies is the alternating perspectives of Heller and Vogel. In the above quote Heller may be piling up his outrage at being abandoned in ways that suggest he is *half* kidding, that there is an ironic tongue lodged in his clenched teeth, but one suspects that a measure of unvarnished truth is also in residence as well. Here, for example, is how Vogel responds to the waves of guilt that followed him out of the room and dogged his heels for a portion of the Gourmet Club's jaunt to Chinatown:

> It was hard to see Joe lying there with food being shoved down his nose while we were taking off for a huge meal. We felt guilty. Mel eased our consciences by reminding us how Heller would behave if the tube was down another's nose. Brooks echoed 'hers who

know Joe well and had seen him recently, saying that even though he looked like a refugee from Dachau, he was a wonderful sick man—maybe the best—and as far as Mel was concerned, Heller could keep that distinction for himself (100).

Moreover, it falls to Vogel, rather than Heller, to cite from the public accounts of the Gourmet Club (in *Playboy,* in *Time,* in *The New Yorker*). The result is that Vogel comes off looking like something of a name-dropper and at times a horn-blower. He not only provides the low-down about the Gourmet Club's elaborate albeit unspoken, rules— e.g., members are nominated and voted on in terms of whether or not they have a "good mouth," a judgment that has everything to do with how they can "pack it in" as eaters and absolutely nothing at all with their ability to make eloquent after-dinner speeches; there is no such thing as ordering "too much" and everybody who thinks that there is could not possibly be a member; and above all else, eating from another person's plate (widely known as sampling) is frowned upon—but he also opens windows on the creative process that are normally nailed shut. In one instance Vogel reveals that he once shared a bachelor pad with Mel Brooks after his marriage hit the rocks, and that Neil Simon turned the comic tales he heard about the arrangement into the Broadway vehicle known as *The Odd Couple.* No doubt Brooks was the model for the neurotic worrywart, Felix Ungar, which leaves Vogel as the model for the lovable slob, Oscar Madison. And it is Vogel who points out how certain Gourmet Club discussions—about why ice flows upstream or why it is good luck that human beings found themselves on a planet that happened to have water—make

their way into the pages of *Good as Gold*. Like James
Joyce, Heller is an author who finds a way to incorporate
stray remarks into the fabric of his fiction. As Vogel remarks, playing Boswell to Heller's Samuel Johnson: "I
am the person who once heard myself saying, 'My mind
is as sharp as a . . . whatamacallit,' a line that popped up
later as dialogue in one of Joe's . . . er . . . whatcha . . .
er . . . books," (35). Joyce often wrote stray phrases or
especially revealing words heard in restaurants on his shirt
cuffs, and then found ways of using them at his writing
desk. No doubt the practice made for uneasy conversation, especially when dinner companions later saw their
words in print. Heller was more subtle about what his ear
and mind took in, but he was no less disarming. The
point, however, is this: Serious students of Heller's fiction
can learn much about his compositional method from the
bon vivant and itinerant herring taster who writes the alternating chapters of *No Laughing Matter*.

At the same time, however, those out for simpler plea-
sures—say, a bit of Mel Brooksiana—will find some
gems strewn through Vogel's chapters. Let this single illustration stand for the many:

> Joe Stein has been eating with us regularly for more
> than ten years. Try though he might, he still cannot
> obtain membership. The late Hershy Kay, the shortest
> man in show business, a composer and the orchestrator
> of such Broadway hits as *Evita* and *A Chorus Line,* ate
> with us for fifteen years and was not a member either.
> For one thing, poor Hershy was much too short for full
> membership (as Mel expressed it, "Except for Joe, all
> of us are quite short. Some of us are very short. Her-
> shy is *too short*.") (104).

Months later—when Heller was well on the road to recovery and installed, along with Vogel and Valerie Humphries, on Fire Island, the gags about Heller's propensity for short friends continued. The Gourmet Club's middle-aged pranksters spared neither others nor themselves:

> This visit from Mel [Brooks], like his first, was a total surprise. All of the guys who showed up that evening were on their way to Chinatown. There were five—Speed, Julie Green, Mel, George Mandel, and Ngoot Lee. Valerie Humphries, as I've said, is tall, perhaps five ten or more. She was flabbergasted to see so many short males enter the room one in back of the other in what for a moment appeared to her to be an endless file, and she did not hesitate to say so. She had never, she exclaimed, seen so many short men in one place. To her merry outcry of astonishment, George Mandel had a benign response.
> "If there were just two more of us," he told her, "you could be Snow White" (231).

If such humor owes much to the Borscht Belt where many of the Gourmet Club members first cut their comedic teeth, one could argue that the most important source for Vogel's persona is probably Huck Finn, or perhaps Saul Bellow's Augie March—that is, some relentlessly puckish spirit who fits most comfortably in the freewheeling conventions of the picaresque novel. Even his ever-present bicycle (which causes him no end of grief when he pedaled over to visit Heller at the hospital on a snowy day when even ordinary means of transportation were perilous and which he later shipped over to Fire Island during the period he stayed there with Heller and Valerie

No Laughing Matter

Humphries) is an emblem of somebody trying, perhaps a bit too hard, a bit too self-consciously, to be Peter Pan. Consider, for example, this moment when Speed is living the "good life" in Capri—courtesy of one sick friend (Heller) and one extremely rich one (Bob Towbin):

> After a good lunch atop Capri, we rode the funicular back to the port and set sail for Brindisi, on the heel of Italy's boot. That was to be our next scheduled stop for fuel, food, and water. We never made it. Just out of Capri, the *Erna* developed a serious engine problem. . . . We were becalmed. . . . We, however, accepted our fate like good sports. We swam, read, ate, drank, sunbathed, and slept soundly. Captain Julian even rigged a rope swing for us to take turns dunking ourselves into the sea. I really did feel like Huck Finn (259).

Granted, given the vision of *No Laughing Matter* as a whole, Vogel is destined to play the role of movement— often frenetic movement—as a foil to Heller's enforced *stasis.* Add the fact that he is a *maven* (expert) about culinary matters, and the result is to tie the gusto of a boy's natural appetite with the voracious "appetites" that characterize the Gourmet Club in general and Joseph Heller in particular.

In such a scheme women are conspicuous by their absence, but *No Laughing Matter* more than makes up for any losses on the plot level by the women who energize and dominate the subplots. Valerie Humphries (who later became the second Mrs. Heller) began as one among many of Heller's nurses, but she soon impressed him by (a) her extraordinarily conscientious care, (b) her uncanny ability to get him talking and talking good talk, and (c) her formidable appetite. No doubt literary ironies played a role as well, because as Heller wooed Valerie with words, he was working on *God Knows,* a novel in which King David, all physical options closed, also depends upon language as a substitute for sexual gratification. As Heller relates the story, a very wise lady once told him that "a man who can talk interestingly to a woman, and especially who can make her laugh, can win her heart" (151). That was precisely the plan he put into action with Valerie Humphries:

> God knows I talked plenty to Valerie and did my best to be interesting. Luckily, I could continue talking away to her a mile a minute even while she was feeding me my breakfast and lunch through the tube, and she could speak to me in turn. (My wise woman could also have added that it helps if the man is willing to listen, but I think that's implied.) . . . Gregarious and jolly instinctively, she soon was displaying a rapt and warm affection for just about everyone she met there through me, and still does (151).

Meanwhile, Vogel, ever the willing alter ego, was sent on missions (escorting Valerie to rock concerts, to the theater, and of course to dinner) as Heller's surrogate. If critics rightly caution those who would read (project?) beyond a novel's final page, the stricture should be doubly binding in the case of a nonfictional account of sickness and recovery such as *No Laughing Matter*. Granted, seriously ill patients often fall in love with their nurses, and the relationship often has its roots in a confusion between "nursing" and "mothering," but the scanty information about Ms Humphries that *No Laugh-*

ing Matter provides is hardly sufficient for a prognosis about their marital future.

What *No Laughing Matter* does make clear, however, what is a matter of "fact," is that Heller was going through a series of painful, protracted divorce proceedings at the same time he was in therapy as a recovering GBS victim. The two themes intersect in ways that bring a number of plots and subplots into congruence: stasis vs. motion, health vs. illness, youth vs. age, dark humor vs. legal formulas. Heller, of course, has a very practiced eye where institutional absurdities are concerned; indeed, nothing more closely binds the vision of his first novel (*Catch-22*) with his most recent (*Picture This*) than a sense that charged words such as *greed* and *power* and *money* have been the levers that move men and history. And as he came to learn—concretely, intimately, existentially—these things also energize divorce proceedings. As Heller puts it in the opening paragraphs of a chapter about his divorce, simply stating the "facts" can sometimes generate the same kind of absurdity that once traveled under the label of the surrealistic:

> Mr. Norman M. Sheresky . . . is listed in the Martindale-Hubbell Law Directory as the author of *Uncoupling—A Guide to Sane Divorce*. In 1978 and 1979, he was president of the New York chapter of the American Academy of Matrimonial Lawyers, and on October 27, 1981, in the Family Court of the State of New York, to which I had been summoned for purposes I still find obscure, he accused me of raping a house.
>
> Now this is no laughing matter (265).

The obsessive attention that Mel Brooks lavished on medical journals and thick books about disease Heller now brought to researches into the law. And in the same spirit that Bruce Gold kept a bulging file on Henry Kissinger in *Good as Gold*—one dumped intact into the novel's pages—Heller paid close attention to lawyers and their penchant for legalese. In short, he carefully designed a naïve persona and a dry, matter-of-fact tone that would not plunge him into deeper, more expensive, legal hot water.

Sheresky does his best to come off as eminently reasonable, as the sort of lawyer trying hard to be cooperative and to settle the matter before him as expeditiously as possible. Heller's attorney is cast as the heavy—as somebody who is both uncooperative and willing to milk Heller's medical condition for all it's worth. As Sheresky puts it in a letter to Jeffrey Cohen, his fellow barrister on the other side of the bench, he dutifully supplied depositions and documents when asked, only to have his own requests go unanswered. Moreover, he will accommodate Heller in as convenient a way as is humanly possible. But try though he might, his letter goes on to say, "you wish to parade Mr. Heller in front of me with nurses and wheelchairs when, believe me, I do not need those props to feel sorry for Mr. Heller and to deeply regret his present physical suffering" (289).

Later, when Heller comes to write this page of *No Laughing Matter* (on 10 March 1981), he mentions that he has heard Sheresky had his own bout with serious illness (he suffered a heart attack and survived)—which prompts him to remark wryly: "I would like the world to know (in the matchless turn of phrase I plagiarize from Gore Vidal, who was writing about Truman Capote

in a context wholly dissimilar) that I feel no less sympathetic to Mr. Sheresky in his illness than he did to me in
mine'' (269).

Meanwhile, back at the bar of justice, Sheresky has
been replaced as attorney by the law firm of Gordon &
Shechtman. Not only would charges that Heller was milk-
ing his exotic condition continue, but William Binderman,
representing Gordon & Shechtman and Mrs. Heller, would
add some interesting new ones to the mix:

> Mr. William N. Binderman was born in Charleston,
> West Virginia, in 1939 and received his law degree
> from Columbia in 1964. He was admitted to the bar in
> 1965, and on July 19, 1983 in the Supreme Court of
> the State of New York, he accused me of writing the
> ''Mein Kampf of matrimonial warfare.''
>
> Naturally, I was surprised (318–19).

Binderman intends to hoist Heller on the petard of his
characters' words, to show that an author can be held le-
gally accountable for his fiction. He tells the judge: Your
Honor, ''Good as Gold'' is a book about an author,
middle-aged author, which as Mr. Heller is, from Coney
Island, with a loyal wife, who goes through what I would
call a middle-age crisis, and plots and schemes throughout
the book to juggle women, conceal his philanderings, plot
and scheme to find a way to conceal all of that from his
wife (320). As a Cliff Notes' outline to *Good as Gold*,
Binderman's characterization leaves a good deal to be de-
sired, but the plot—and the attendant ironies—thicken
when he actually introduces what he thinks are relevant
citations from Heller's fiction into the court proceedings.
Here, courtesy of Heller, is how the actual transcript reads
at this point:

Q: Are these the words of Joseph Heller, "I want a divorce, I need a divorce, I crave a divorce, I pray for a divorce, all my life I have wanted a divorce, even before I was married.". . . You wrote those words in *Good as Gold*, didn't you, Mr. Heller?

A: No.

Mr. Binderman was quoting from my novel *Something Happened*. And that was just about it for his foundation for my *Mein Kampf* (322).

That laugh may have come at Binderman's expense, and no doubt Heller enjoyed it mightily; nonetheless, when the bills for Heller's various legal services rolled in, the effect was radically different from, say, the check one gets at the end of a great meal. Heller's divorce was time-consuming and physically draining. It was also expensive:

Mr. Felder, as I've said, received $70,000 at the end and at least $10,000 earlier, of which $35,000 came from me. Mr. Sheresky and the Gordon firm separately asked for $50,000 and settled for $25,000, of which my share was $17,500 for each, and my wife's share was $7,500.

A final payment by me to Jeffrey of $20,000 brought the amount paid him over three years to $100,000; one of us may owe the other a few thousand, but neither of us wishes to find out which.

And Sidney, as I knew in suggesting him as someone acceptable to both sides, does not work for little. His bill was close to $40,000 for the six or seven months spent, of which $25,000 came from me, and the rest was due him from my wife. (322–23).

The litany of Heller's mounting legal expenses is worth citing at some length because Heller details his financial woes with the same attention to fact, and the same sense of utter surprise, that had characterized his account of his medical condition and its various treatments. In a book largely about one man's encounter with GBS, the cost system of American medicine brought the tab to something in the $100,000 range. By contrast, his divorce, when the costs of lawyers and accountants were reckoned, exceeds the $300,000 mark—all for what Heller describes as "a divorce I earnestly believe neither my wife nor I wanted." With that bitter line Heller's contribution to the book comes to an end.

But in Speed Vogel's final chapter he points out that Heller is "now the most patient and considerate of men." He not only jumps at the chance for evenings out, but also finds himself receiving—and answering—correspondence from fellow GBS sufferers. Moreover, Vogel had never seen anyone *a zoi fahliebed* (Yiddish for "so much in love"). Indeed, *paradox* may be the only way to describe Heller's newfound sense of well-being and happiness. In a puckish fantasy Vogel imagines Heller resting his massive head on Vogel's shoulder, the body of an old friend suddenly going slack: "With a peaceful smile, he turned his face toward mine and softly murmured, 'It's been such a wonderful year.' . . . Slowly his eyes fell closed and he died in my arms" (334).

Not surprisingly, Heller objects to Vogel's outrageous exercise in the melodramatic and just plain cornball. Such guys should have their poetic licenses revoked:

> I did no such thing. What the hell's the matter with him? I have no recollection whatsoever of dying in his arms and I don't know why the damned fool keeps insisting that I did. What I did do that evening was enjoy a hearty dinner of the pot roast he cooked, and a few weeks later I flew down to Florida to visit my brother

and sister, largely to prove to them and to myself that I was now able to travel alone (334).

And while it is true that the book ends with him moving slowly and cautiously, with him still having some difficulties with speech (l's are particularly troublesome, especially for a man with two of them in his surname), he is, in most other respects, "a great guy" (335). And as for those who might wonder about the effect of the disease on his sexual powers,

> I report with some regret [and more than a little tongue in cheek] that the improvement is barely measureable and that I am no better now at satisfying a romantic woman than I was before. Recommended alternatives to Guillain-Barré in this area are ginseng root, the dried cantharides beetle, and powdered rhinoceros horn. Avoid wishful thinking. It hardly ever does the trick (335).

Thus far, *Picture This* is the only book he has written since his bout with GBS and the extended therapy that attended his recovery, but Heller continues to keep the fires of interest alive by hinting that a sequel to *Catch-22* is in the works. One thing, however, is clear: if Heller's estimates of how much his disease and his divorce cost are even half right, he is likely to be spending the better part of next few decades at the writing desk.

NOTE

1. Heller and Speed Vogel, *No Laughing Matter* (New York: Putnam's, 1986) 7-8. Subsequent references are to this edition and are noted parenthetically.

CHAPTER SEVEN

Picture This

The advance notices about *Picture This* were hardly encouraging; indeed, one library service called the novel "pretentious, unimaginative, and tedious." But even those who branded the book a dud were quick to add that, given Heller's enormous reputation, "demand" (something librarians care about) was a certainty. After all, *Picture This* was a Book-of-the-Month Club featured alternate, and *any* book by Heller was certain to be reviewed in all the wide-circulation popular magazines.

As it turned out, however, the best one could say for the first round of reviews is that they were deferential. As Walter Goodman put it in *The New York Times*:

> Why should Joseph Heller have written a book about the life of Rembrandt and the death of Socrates, the rise of the Netherlands and the fall of Athens? As the narrator shrugs, in one of the many punchlines that keep reminding us of the author's presence, "Don't ask me."[1]

Robert M. Adams felt much the same way in the Sunday *New York Times Book Review*, adding that Heller gave him the impression of garnering the material about the worlds of Aristotle and Rembrandt from first-rate sources, "and as for being irrelevant to one another, or to anything else in particular, that was evidently part of the comic intent. So I would say it represents very spacedout writing. It may be funny as well, and for all I know it's awesome."[2] What no magazine or newspaper wanted to do, however, was give the book more than "polite" space—and in this case the editorial decision also suited the reviewers. Even those paid by the word weren't sure what "words" could be applied to this sprawling meditation on world history.

Heller had drawn deeply from historical material before (in *God Knows*), but *Picture This* somehow seems more strained and more taxing, not only because its coverage is so panoramic, but also because its authorial voice is at once insistent and dryly matter of fact. The result seems more akin to a textbook (albeit one rendered from a bitterly satirical perspective) than a novel. As the Bob Slocum of *Something Happened* points out during one of few times when "instruction" replaces shouting matches, "Money makes social studies. Without money there would be no social studies." Moreover, this is one of the few times when his daughter not only agrees with Slocum, but also goes on to amplify his remark: "What Dad means . . . is that the love of money and the quest for gold and riches in the past is what caused most of the events we read about today in all our history books" (440). Granted, Slocum is no less monstrous about money than he is about nearly everything else. For him "money is everything" (indeed, that is why it is unthinkable that his son so blithely gives his nickels away). And when confronted with the canard that money can't buy health, he simply turns the old saw on its head: health can't buy money. In *Picture This* money is not only the root of sociopolitical evil, but also the wellspring of art. The difference between the two books, however, is the difference between the deadly serious (*Picture This*) and the darkly seriocomic (*Something Happened*).

Other comparisons with the Heller canon also come to mind. Take *God Knows*, for example. No doubt even those who thought that that novel contained far too much Catskill humor would have welcomed some of its comic relief during the extended sections when *Picture This* provides more minutiae about the Netherlands or about ancient Greece than most readers wanted to know. Part of the difference can be chalked up to "research," and more important, to how research was incorporated into the respective books. In *God Knows*, Heller took the biblical King David as a starting point, but allowed himself a free hand to make his protagonist appropriately "contemporary." By contrast, *Picture This* is heavy with effortfulness. As Heller makes clear in the acknowledgments, a wide variety of scholars contributed to the making of *Picture This*: Gary Schwartz, art historian and publisher "whose newest book on Rembrandt was of immeasurable value to me"; Simon Schama, author of *The Embarrassment of Riches*; Lillian Feder, a classicist who teaches at City University; and a second Gary Schwartz, a classicist at Lehman College, "who corrected my mistakes, refined my classical vocabulary." Unfortunately, the result is a case of too much unassimilated information using Heller, rather than the other way around. In an effort to get things "right," the book suffers from an imaginative shortfall.

In the language of fashionable literary criticism *Picture This* is an extended exercise in deconstruction— that is, a self-conscious effort which calls determinant meanings into question and which regards the text as a closed verbal system. Thus, the *meaning* of a work of art (to say nothing of its applicability to life) becomes problematic. In such a view structure is more likely to undermine "meaning" than to buttress it, and a closer look at the elements of a given text is more likely to unearth subtexts that cancel each other out rather than contribute to a unified, coherent whole. In short, deconstruction turned literature into a highly complicated linguistic game. Heller, of course, writes as a novelist, but something of the same spirit that clusters around much being thought and said by literary theorists can be applied to *Picture This*. For example, the novel begins by "contemplating" Rembrandt's famous painting *Aristotle Contemplating the Bust of Homer* and ends by dismantling its component parts:

> The Rembrandt painting of Aristotle contemplating the bust of Homer may not be by Rembrandt but by a pupil so divinely gifted in learning the lessons of his master that he never was able to accomplish anything more and whose name, as a consequence, has been lost in obscurity. The bust of Homer that Aristotle is shown contemplating is not of Homer. The man is not Aristotle.[3]

Thus, Heller is out to "demystify" (yet another charged, fashionable critical word) a painting whose fame—and price—far outstrips its aesthetic value. But for all of Heller's painstaking attention to the details that surround the "composition" of Aristotle and the bust of Homer, as well as of Rembrandt and the socioeconomic conditions of seventeenth-century Holland, the issues in *Picture This* ripple well beyond questions of illusion and reality, art and life. For *Picture This* means to unload an eyeful about the greed and crimes of history and perhaps even more, by analogy, about "now."

Consider, for example, the opening paragraphs of chapter 2:

> Rembrandt painting Aristotle contemplating the bust of Homer was himself contemplating the bust of Homer as it stood on the red cloth covering the square table in the left foreground and wondering how much money it might fetch at the public auction of his belongings that he was already contemplating was sooner or later going to be more or less inevitable.
>
> Aristotle could have told him it would not fetch much. The bust of Homer was a copy.
>
> It was an authentic Hellenic imitation of a Hellenic reproduction of a statue for which there had never been an authentic original subject (4).

Heller's style has always been partial to the oxymoronic ("authentic imitation of a Hellenic reproduction") and the possibilities that result when one pushes an observation to its logical absurdity. Heller might argue that he is simply recording the facts of the matter, but those who have followed the arc of his career know better; Rembrandt's painting is for Heller what a "found object" is to certain contemporary poets—namely, the objectification of a world view. That things are not as they seem—that the bust is not of Homer, nor is the representation of Aristotle really Aristotle—becomes merely the tip of a much larger iceberg. Indeed, *nothing* is as it appears, although if the Big Lie is repeated long enough, the illusion not only is regarded as the truth, but people are perfectly happy to pay enormous amounts of money for it. Meanwhile, Socrates would have laughed at "this imitation on canvas in color of this copy in plaster or stone of an imitation in marble of the likeness of a man whom nobody we know of had ever seen and of whose existence there is no reliable written or oral verification (34). Such tangled sentences abound in *Picture This*, partly as an expression of Heller's elevated point of view, but also as a means of generating curmudgeonly humor.

At one level *Picture This* is the increasingly complicated story of the making of an illusion—namely, Rembrandt's *Aristotle Contemplating the Bust of Homer*. And as such, the book becomes an extended exercise in reflexivity, rather like Bruce Gold's efforts to write a book about the American-Jewish experience in *Good as Gold*. But whereas *Good as Gold* suffered from too many disparate plot lines, *Picture This* virtually abandons the usual expectations about character, setting, and plot. What readers get instead is the process of painterly composition; a survey of histories ancient, post-Renaissance, and modern; and most of all, a meditation on what art and life eventually come to. There are heavy burdens to place on readers who thought their $19.95 was buying a comic novel by the author of *Catch-22*.

That said, it might be helpful to think of painterly composition as a series of questions, and of strategies designed to answer them. At what point, Heller muses, does a blob of paint on a canvas become more than a certain arrangement of color, position, and texture? Indeed, at what point does art *become* Life, or conversely, at what point does life manifest itself most tellingly in art? In short, when does "representation" become the thing itself? Consider, for example, this instance of dramatic change as Rembrandt gives the Aristotle on his canvas (who, of course, is not modeled on Aristotle at all, but rather on a seventeenth-century Dutch citizen "playing" the role of Aristotle) an ear:

> Aristotle could hear, of course, after Rembrandt gave him an ear—and then to his enormous surprise and glee, adorned it with an earring whose worth, were it fabricated of real gold instead of simulated with paint, would have been more than nominal in the jewelry markets of the city. And Aristotle heard enough to understand that the artist creating him had more on his mind than completing this particular canvas for Don Antonio Ruffo and the several other paintings in the studio on which he was also working (11).

In a poem or short story the focus would no doubt have stayed on the painting of Aristotle—first ears, then eyes, etc., until Aristotle, like Browning's Last Duchess, comes *alive* on the wall. And no doubt because Heller has chosen something like Chinese boxes to begin with—with one box opening to a smaller box and then to another— one supposes that the relationship between Rembrandt and his painting would be mirrored by the relationship of Aristotle to Homer. But Heller means to set each of these possibilities within a much wider historical-cultural context. Roughly the same literary technique applies to Heller's analysis of Rembrandt's *The Jewish Bride*, a painting in which "almost everything seems wrong in a picture that is absolutely right":

> The man and woman look funny. We don't know who they are, or the year the painting was completed, or why it is called *The Jewish Bride*. They are not thinking of each other. Neither relates to the

viewer. . . . They are lost in thought in worlds apart. No interpretation yet advanced of this monument in pictorial art makes sense. We don't know who these two people are, or who they are supposed to be, or what they are doing there. We don't even know that they are married, and neither the man nor the woman looks any more Jewish than you or I (242).

For Heller art requires a sociopolitical context—even if, as is the case with *Aristotle Contemplating the Bust of Homer*, the context turns suspect on closer examination. Thus, chapter 3 begins with Aristotle at sixty-two, reflecting on the death of Socrates, and at something of a dead end:

> Among the many things he knew toward the end of his life was that there were many more he did not.
> A thing he did not know, of course, was that in the Dutch Republic in the seventeenth century, Rembrandt would paint his picture in Amsterdam, and that for close to two hundred years just about no one in the world would know who he was (15).

Aristotle thus becomes the anchoring point around which discussions of Plato and Socrates, the Age of Pericles, and the Peloponnesian War revolve. Heller's sources include Thucydides, Plutarch, and other scholarly accounts of the classical world. One also suspects that Heller has also made good use of reference tools such as the *Timetables of History*, as the following passage suggests:

> Socrates was past forty when Plato was born.
> He was more than sixty when they met, and Plato could not have known for as many as ten years the man

who was to inspire him with a lifelong devotion to thought and whose death was to embitter him with a disillusioned hatred for the political freedom and materialistic orientation of the democratic city with which both names are associated.

That age of Pericles, which we think of now as the golden age of Athens, came to an end, literally, with the death of Pericles in the second of the twenty-seven years of war into which that most sensible and constructive of political leaders guided his city inflexibly toward total defeat, unconditional surrender, and the loss of power and empire. That was the year of the plague, transported by sea from the upper Nile into the walled city besieged on land for the second summer in a row by Spartan soldiers and Spartan allies. Pericles, already wretched from parliamentary setbacks inflicted on him by the conservative nobility on one side and the radical business community on the other, and by a series of personal tragedies too, was himself among the tens of thousands who fell victim to the disease and died (17).

Heller's point, of course, is that history is more interconnected than most chronological accounts would suggest. Moreover, histories not only repeat themselves, but they do so in rather predictable ways. For example, when Plato suggests that mercantile societies tend to be "quarrelsome and litigious" (10), the observation turns out to be true not only for the seventeenth-century society of which Rembrandt himself was a litigious member, but also for the contemporary American society that made such a fuss when his painting of *Aristotle Contemplating the Bust of Homer* was sold to the Metropolitan Museum of Art in 1961 for a (then) record amount of $2,300,000.

Then, as now, the best-laid plans of those in power have a way not only of going awry, but also of ending in absurdity: "Pericles believed the war would be short. Sparta would see in one year that victory was impossible and accede to a peace without the concessions demanded earlier. The strategy of Pericles was flawless. The strategy failed" (143). Heller's droll one-liners are meant to carry the snap and satiric punch associated with American literature at its best—with the acerbic social commentary of Melville's *The Confidence Man* or the debunking portraits that John Dos Passos sprinkles throughout his *USA* trilogy. At the same time, however, *Picture This* is a history with an important difference; namely, the use of loaded, contemporary phrases (e.g., "cold war" or "police state") to describe events during the Age of Pericles:

> Neither radicals nor conservatives thought much of democracy as a viable form of government.
> They still don't.
> Reactionary warmongers calling themselves neocon-servatives deserted the democrats of Pericles to join the aristocrats, and were despised by both parties.
> He [Pericles] was never accused of homosexuality.
> He was accused of heterosexuality (139).

Here Heller's effort by way of relevance serves to tip his hand. This is, unashamedly, historiography with an agenda. And lest there be those who get lost in the tangles of intention and result that brought ancient Athens to its knees, Heller is more than delighted to break into his narrative to make sure contemporary readers get the point:

> From Athens to Syracuse by oar and sail was just about equivalent to the journey by troopship today from

California to Vietnam, or from Washington, D.C., to the Beirut airport in Lebanon or to the Persian Gulf.

Do not make war in a hostile distant land unless you intend to live there.

The people will outnumber you, your presence will be alarming, the government you install to keep order will not keep order, victory is impossible if the people keep fighting, there is only genocide to cope with determined local military resistance (198).

Moreover, should the extended analogy fail to drive home the point—although it's hard to imagine anyone missing it—Heller makes his position on the continuing absurdity of governments abundantly clear. Pericles was not the only one who lived in the disastrous Age of Pericles; in their own bumbling way our leaders are more than a match for the Pericles whose strategies ended in abject failure. The only difference is that American leaders have grown a good deal more sophisticated in hiding what they do behind the smoke screens of a terminology George Orwell earlier identified as doublespeak:

After World War II, in 1947, the U.S. Department of War, an institution of American government since 1789, was abolished and subsequently reconstituted as the Department of Defense; the Secretary of War was renamed the Secretary of Defense.

And from that day to the present, the United States of America was never again in danger of war.

It was in danger of defense (262).

Language is nearly always the first casualty of efforts to organize people to fight wars or to believe that their lives are better served by collective hands, whether those hands belong to the government or to the corporation.

By way of illustration Heller reminds us that "it was only with the death of Pericles that true democracy came at last to Athens"—and with it, the eternal conflict that pits freedom and free enterprise against one another:

> Democracy and free enterprise go hand in hand and are unfriendly to each other. They go hand in hand and are deadly enemies, for the only freedom business cares about is the freedom to do business. The desire for justice doesn't count (152).

Heller has made the cause of justice his highest priority. In this sense he writes within the prophetic tradition of Isaiah and Jeremiah, something that critics had first noticed when they turned their attention to *Catch-22*. But so relentless, so insistent, is *Picture This* about evil's conspiratorial nature that common readers are in some danger of being overwhelmed by the assault. As Heller's view of history would have it, thus has it been ever. Like Rembrandt's painting, *Picture This* is a portrait etched in the darkest possible hues. And while it is true that the narrative voice is always dryly matter of fact as it alternates among a wide range of historical setting, it is also true that the sound of Heller's gritted teeth is never entirely absent. Here, for example, sandwiched between a section concerning Pericles' legislation barring Megaran ships from Athenian ports and a discussion of the 1652 battle of The Downs, is a barb aimed at Lyndon Johnson:

> "We make war that we may live in peace," said Lyndon Johnson, quoting Aristotle, who was embarrassed, and paraphrasing Adolf Hitler.
>
> The desire of some men for peace is a frequent cause of war (122).

Unfortunately, there are not only too many places in *Picture This* where Heller indulges his white-hot indignation, but also far too many occasions when he clearly regards his analyses as carrying more philosophical weight than they actually do.

However, Heller's *real* point—buried beneath piles of research but transparent all the same—is actually a fairly simple, and largely apolitical, one: namely, that then, as now, money talks; and that this is true whether one is speaking about commerce, about conquest, or, yes, even about art:

> To Aristotle contemplating the bust of Homer, the continuing preoccupation of the world with making money remained an enigma he was not even aware he was unable to decipher. . . . Homer begged and Rembrandt went bankrupt, Aristotle, who had money for books, his school and his museum, could not have bought this painting of himself.
> Rembrandt could not afford a Rembrandt (59–60).

Unjust is the charged word of *Picture This*, just as it is the charged word of nearly every Heller work with the curious exception of *No Laughing Matter*. And even in *No Laughing Matter*—where humor turns out to be a better survival technique than railing about the injustice of disease—divorce lawyers turn out to be "unjust," and very costly.

For the Rembrandt that Heller "creates" in *Picture This*, not only grinding poverty is unjust, but also the realization that his dunce of a pupil, Govert Flinck, gets more money for his imitations of Rembrandt than he can get for an original. The result, of course, is tailor-made for a snatch of Heller's absurdist theater, a typical piece of Heller *shtick* that pits a naïf against those in the know:

> "What you're [the model for Aristotle in Rembrandt's famous painting] wearing is plated. The ring, the earring, the rest. The chain is an imitation in brass. Come closer. Look at the chain and look at the picture. Don't you see the difference? This gold is real."
>
> The gold on the canvas looked the more authentic.
>
> "I don't think I want to talk about it," the man said unhappily. "You speak of imitation," he said tentatively, and fell silent, considering whether to say more. "Do you know that Govert Flinck is becoming more and more successful with paintings he did that are imitations of yours, of you and your style?". . .
>
> "That makes no sense. He gets more for his imitations of my work than I do for my originals?"
>
> "They're more in demand."
>
> "Why should they be? Why should people pay more money to him for his old imitations of my work when they can buy my original paintings from me?"
>
> "They say his are better" (182–83).

One reads such lines and agrees: unjust, unjust—especially since Heller has earlier taken the bother to reproduce, and comment on, the handful of surviving Rembrandt letters that natter on about money. What's a poor, "original" genius like Rembrandt to do in a world that prefers copies? Moreover, when his model tells him that Flinck's "surfaces are smooth, his colors are transparent, his lines define forms, his details are precise," Rembrandt loudly insists that that's *not* his style: "Flinck is an imposter. I don't paint that way." In short, one's worst nightmare thus comes true—namely, that you are "copied" and, what is worse, copied badly. The erstwhile Rembrandt is not really Rembrandt—he lacks Rembrandt's sense of technique, and more important, his consummate genius—but Flinck soon becomes the measure of what a Rembrandt must now "copy." Which, of course, is where Rembrandt's advice-giver (and Heller's exercise in absurdic logic) leads: namely, to the only conclusion "logically" possible in such a world:

> "Then perhaps you ought to," counseled Six with a smile, "if you want to regain your popularity and get prices like his."
> "And then," said Rembrandt with a sneer, "my paintings would be copies of his imitations of my originals, wouldn't they?"
> "Exactly," Six agreed. "Especially if he went back to painting like you. Best of all, you would not have to spend time doing any more originals, would you?"
> "And what name should I sign to them? Mine or his?"
> "You'd make more money, I think, if you signed them with his. Or, if you like, perhaps you can persuade Flinck to sign the name of Rembrandt to yours" (184–85).

No doubt there are those who will see this as an instance of postmodernism at its most inventive and most provocative—rather like the playful fictions-about-fiction that characterize the work of John Barth, Robert Coover, and others in the school of metafiction. But taken as a whole, *Picture This* reminds one more of the embittered, aging Mark Twain who had soured on life and had begun to think of himself as a serious philosopher rather than a "mere humorist." Rewriting the respective "histories" of

Adam and Eve or revealing, via his "mysterious stranger," that all of life is but a dreamy illusion gave Twain the slim excuse he needed to vent his frustrations, and he could not unload his dark visions fast enough. Heller engages in much the same sophomoric ranting in *Picture This*:

> There are outrages and there are outrages, and some are more outrageous than others.
>
> Mankind is resilient: the atrocities that horrified us a week ago become acceptable tomorrow.
>
> The death of Socrates had no effect upon the history of Athens. If anything, the reputation of the city had been improved by it.
>
> The death of no person is as important to the future as the literature about it.
>
> You will learn nothing from history that can be applied, so don't kid yourself into thinking it can.
>
> "History is bunk," said Henry Ford.
>
> But Socrates was dead.
>
> Plato does not report that he wept that day (340).

The argument of *Picture This*—namely, that the more things change, the more they remain the same—has ambition and scope, enormous effort, and not a few examples of the dazzling cadences and satiric wit associated with Joseph Heller at his novelistic best. But it is also true that the book is awash with large chunks of material drawn virtually unchanged from the Socratic dialogues and Plato's *Laws*, from Aristotle and Thucydides, from political histories of seventeenth-century Holland, and biographies of Rembrandt van Rijn. Thus, *Picture This* is not only about imitation—as Plato and Aristotle and Rembrandt defined the term; it is itself an imitation of an

Picture This

imitation of an imitation. The result is not only a book that reveals more about the Age of Pericles, about Rembrandt's tangled finances, or about the strange odyssey that brought *Aristotle Contemplating the Bust of Homer* to the auction block than it does about the painting, or about literature, per se. Both Rembrandt's portrait *and* Heller's book are effectively "deconstructed" in the process.

What *Picture This* does have, however, is the uncompromising language and the satiric vision that have been Heller's trademarks. As the narrator, quoting Thucydides, puts it: "Language was debased. The ordinary acceptance of words in their relation to things was changed as men saw fit" (167). Heller has been particularly aware of this condition as it manifests itself in military-industrial complexes, in bureaucracies, and, as his latest book makes abundantly clear, in everything from Plato's admonitions against "imitation" to Rembrandt's painting of *Aristotle Contemplating the Bust of Homer*.

Heller's career thus far has been a rare instance of nothing quite succeeding like a spectacular success. That that success—*Catch-22*—was his first novel has not come without a certain cost (how could his subsequent books be regarded as anything but disappointments?). But he is still regarded both as a major American fictionist and as a enormously popular writer. Moreover, there are those who confidently predict that *Something Happened* will one day be regarded as Heller's finest, most important achievement, although the steady sales of *Catch-22*—generation after generation—make this an unlikely bet. About Heller's other books there is less disagreement and considerably less enthusiasm.

One thing, however, is clear: Heller continues to write novels. And if William Faulkner's view that fictionists ought to be judged by their interesting "failures" is correct, then Heller may yet become known as more than the writer who added "catch-22" to our national vocabulary. After all, he did not merely repeat the successes of *Catch-22*, impressive as they clearly were. Instead, his fiction is characterized by a willingness to chart new territories and new techniques. The result has been a marvelous capacity to take on new subjects—everything from King David to Rembrandt to Henry Kissinger—and to do so in ways that are hardly lacking in ambition, in scope, or in deadly comic accuracy. Given such a disposition, more surprises, and more delights, no doubt await his many readers.

NOTES

1. Walter Goodman, "Heller Contemplating Rembrandt . . . ," *The New York Times* 1 Sept. 1988: C-32

2. Robert M. Adams, "History Is a Bust," *New York Times Book Review* 4 Sept. 1988: 15.

3. Heller, *Picture This* (New York: Putnam's, 1988) 341. Subsequent references are to this edition and are noted parenthetically.

BIBLIOGRAPHY

Works by Joseph Heller

NOVELS

Catch 22. New York: Simon and Schuster, 1961; London: Cape, 1962.
Something Happened. New York: Knopf, 1974; London: Cape, 1974.
Good as Gold. New York: Simon and Schuster, 1979; London: Cape, 1979.
God Knows. New York: Knopf, 1984.
Picture This. New York: Putnam's, 1988.

MEMOIRS

No Laughing Matter (co-author, Speed Vogel). New York: Putnam's, 1986.

PLAYS

We Bombed in New Haven. Yale School of Drama, New Haven, 4 December 1967; Ambassador Theatre, New York, 16 October 1968. New York: Knopf, 1968; London: Cape, 1969.
Catch-22: A Dramatization. New York: French, 1971.
Clevinger's Trial. New York: French, 1973; London: Cape, 1974.

SCREENPLAYS

Sex and the Single Girl, by Heller and David R. Schwartz. Warner Bros., 1964.
Dirty Dingus Magee, by Heller and others. MGM, 1970.

Bibliography

OTHER

"Catch 18." *New World Writing No. 7* (New York: New American Library, 1955). 204–14.

"World Full of Great Cities." *Nelson Algren's Own Book of Lonesome Monsters.* New York: Lander, 1964.

PERIODICAL PUBLICATIONS

"I Don't Love You Any More." *Story* 28 (Sept./Oct. 1945): 40–45.

"Castle of Snow." *Atlantic Monthly* Mar. 1948: 52–55.

"Girl from Greenwich." *Esquire* June 1948: 40–41, 142–43.

"A Man Named Flute." *Atlantic Monthly* Aug. 1948: 66–70.

"Nothing to Be Done." *Esquire* Aug. 1948: 73, 129–30.

"McAdam's Log." *Gentleman's Quarterly* Dec. 1959: 112, 166–76, 178.

"Too Timid to Damn, Too Stingy to Applaud." *New Republic* 30 July 1962: 23–24, 26.

"Coney Island: The FUN Is Over," *Show* 10 July 1962: 50–54; 102–03.

"Catch 22 Revisited." *Holiday* April 1967: 44–61.

"How I Found James Bond." *Holiday* June 1967: 123–25.

"Love, Dad." *Playboy* Dec. 1969: 181–82, 348.

INTERVIEWS

Amos, Martin. "Joseph Heller in Conversation with Martin Amos." *New Review* 2 (1975): 55–59.

Barnard, Ken. "Joseph Heller Tells How *Catch-18* Became *Catch-22* and Why He Was Afraid of Airplanes." *Detroit News* 13 Sept. 1970: 19, 24, 27–28, 30, 65.

Gross, Martin L. "Conversation with an Author." *Book Digest* May, 1976: 14–15, 20–23.

Krassner, Paul. "An Impolite Interview with Joseph Heller." *The Realist* Nov. 1962: 18–26, 28–31.

Merrill, Sam. "Playboy Interview: Joseph Heller." *Playboy* June 1975: 59–61, 64–66, 68, 70, 72–74, 76.

Plimpton, George. "The Art of Fiction LI: Joseph Heller." *Paris Review* 60 (1974): 126–47.

Sale, Richard. "An Interview in New York with Joseph Heller." *Studies in the Novel* 4 (1972): 63–74.

Shapiro, James. "Work in Progress: Joseph Heller, an Interview." *Intellectual Digest* 2 (1971): 6–11.

Bibliography

Whitman, Alden. "Something Always Happens on the Way to the Office: An Interview with Joseph Heller." *Pages: The World of Books, Writers and Writings,* vol. 1. Ed. Matthew J. Bruccoli and C. E. Frazer Clark, Jr. Detroit: Gale, 1976. 74–81.

Critical Works about Heller

BIBLIOGRAPHIES

Keegan, Brenda M. *Joseph Heller: A Reference Guide.* Boston: Hall, 1978.

Scotto, Robert M. *Three Contemporary Novelists: An Annotated Bibliography of Works by and about John Hawkes, Joseph Heller, and Thomas Pynchon.* New York: Garland, 1977.

Weixmann, Joseph. "A Bibliography of Joseph Heller's *Catch-22.*" *Bulletin of Bibliography* 31 (1974): 32–37.

COLLECTIONS OF CRITICISM

Kiley, Frederick, and Walter McDonald, eds. *A Catch-22 Casebook.* New York: Crowell, 1973. An important collection of essays and reviews. Contains several original essays and a previously unpublished interview with Heller.

Nagel, James, ed. *Critical Essays on "Catch-22."* Encino, CA: Dickenson, 1974. Includes several original essays of enduring value. Useful annotated bibliography.

———. *Critical Essays on Joseph Heller.* Boston: Hall, 1984. Major essays on each of Heller's works, including plays, through *Good as Gold.* Introduction is a most useful bibliographic guide to Heller's scholarship.

Scotto, Robert M., ed. *"Catch-22": A Critical Edition.* New York: Delta, 1973. Several critical studies as well as the text of *Catch-22.*

ARTICLES AND SECTIONS OF BOOKS

Aldridge, John W. *The American Novel and the Way We Live Now.* New York: Oxford University Press, 1983. 35–46. Challenging readings of *Something Happened* and *Good as Gold* as embodying Heller's "nihilistic perception."

Alter, Robert. "The Apocalyptic Temper." *Commentary* June, 1966: 61–66. Discusses *Catch 22* and other modern novels in light of Jewish theological traditions.

Bibliography

Brewer, Joseph E. "The Anti-Hero in Contemporary Literature." *Iowa English Bulletin* 12 (1967): 55–60. Places *Catch-22* in a modern movement which uses the anti-hero as protagonist.

Bryant, Jerry H. *The Open Decision: The Contemporary American Novel and Its Intellectual Background.* New York: Free Press, 1970. 156–64. Discusses the thematic implications of Yossarian's flight to Sweden.

Burhans, Clinton S., Jr. "Spindrift and the Sea: Structural Patterns and Unifying Elements in *Catch-22*." *Twentieth Century Literature* 19 (1973): 239–50. Rpt. Nagel, *Critical Essays on Joseph Heller.* Helpful in demonstrating the chronological and structural integrity of Heller's first novel. Especially good on the book's "tonal structure."

Cheuse, Alan. "Laughing on the Outside." *Studies on the Left* 3 (1963): 81–87. Argues that *Catch-22* is weakened by sentimentality.

Costa, Richard Hauer. "Notes from a Dark Heller: Bob Slocum and the Underground Man." *Texas Studies in Literature and Language* 23 (1981): 159–82. Comparison of Heller's and Dostoevski's "heroes." One of the better psychological studies of Slocum.

Day, Douglass. "*Catch-22:* A Manifesto for Anarchists." *Carolina Quarterly* 15 (1963): 86–92. Concludes that *Catch-22* is a "mass of tastelessness and vulgarity" and a "blowzy, careening, cliché-ridden, fly-specked sort of monstrosity."

Davis, Gary W. "Catch-22 and the Language of Discontinuity." *Novel* 12 (1978): 66–77. Rpt. Nagel, *Critical Essays on Joseph Heller.* Sensitive to Heller's linguistic "absurdities," but inclined to see them as mirroring an absurd universe.

Del Fattore, Joan. "The Dark Stranger in Heller's *Something Happened.*" Nagel, *Critical Essays on Joseph Heller.* 127–38. An acute psychological reading that focuses on Slocum's recurring dreams.

Friedman, John and Judith Ruderman. "Joseph Heller and the 'Real' King David," *Judaism* 36 (1987): 296–301.

Doskow, Minna. "The Night Journey in *Catch-22*." *Twentieth Century Literature* 12 (1967): 186–93. Rpt. Nagel, *Critical Essays on "Catch-22."* Focuses on "The Eternal City" chapter in *Catch-22.*

Friedman, Melvin J. "Something Jewish Happened: Some Jewish Thoughts about Joseph Heller's *Good as Gold.*" Nagel, *Critical Essays on Joseph Heller.* 196–204. Knowledgable in its discussion of *Good as Gold* and recent Jewish-American fiction. Good suggestions as to where Heller positions himself within this literary context.

Galloway, David D. "Clown and Saint: The Hero in Current American Fiction." *Critique* 7 (1965): 46–65. Sees the contemporary American aesthetic as a result of the development of an urban society. The war in *Catch-22* is a metaphor for dehumanization and Yossarian's struggle for survival makes him representative of modern man.

Gaukroger, Doug. "Time Structure in *Catch-22*." *Critique* 12 (1967): 46–57.

Greenfield, Josh. "22 Was Funnier than 14." *New York Times Book Review* 3 Mar. 1968: 1, 49–51, 53. Covers the publishing history of the novel to 1968. Sees as the central theme the "exquisite totalitarianism" of the military and concludes that the novel is not as bold as it seems, although still a major work.

Harris, Charles B. "*Catch-22*: A Radical Protest against Absurdity." *Contemporary American Novelists of the Absurd*. New Haven: College and University Press, 1971. 33–50. The first clear recognition that *Catch-22* does not embrace the theme of cosmic absurdity.

Henry, G. B. Mck. "Significant Corn: *Catch-22*." *Melbourne Critical Review* 9 (1966): 133–44. An examination of the satire and "cinematic visualization" of the novel which finds the ending to be inconsistent with the "power" and "logic" of the rest of the book.

Karl, Frederick R. "Joseph Heller's *Catch-22*: Only Fools Walk in Darkness." *Contemporary American Novelists*, ed. Harry T. Moore. Carbondale: Southern Illinois University Press, 1965. 134–42. Reads the novel as social satire which is essentially optimistic.

Kazin, Alfred. "The War Novel: From Mailer to Vonnegut." *Saturday Review* 6 Feb. 1971: 13–15, 36. Sees war as insane and Yossarian as a sane man who wants only to survive.

Kennard, Jean. "Joseph Heller: At War with Absurdity." *Mosaic* 4 (1971): 75–87. Argues that the style, narrative method, tone, and characterization all serve to frustrate the reader's expectations so that *Catch-22* becomes the experience of the absurd.

LeClair, Thomas. "Joseph Heller, *Something Happened*, and the Art of Excess." *Studies in American Fiction* 9 (1981): 245–60. Rpt. Nagel, *Critical Essays on Joseph Heller*. Probably the most sensitive reading of Heller's second novel, though tied to its curiously limited thesis that Heller meant to expose "the ultimate futility of quantitative and casual thinking."

Bibliography

Lowin, Joseph. "The Jewish Art of Joseph Heller." *Jewish Book Annual* 43 (1985–86): 141–53. The first published essay on *God Knows*. A defense of Heller's sympathetic treatment of the Judaic tradition.

McDonald, James L. "I See Everything Twice: The Structure of Joseph Heller's *Catch-22*." *University Review* 34 (1968): 175–80. Argues that the novel achieves structural unity through the use of *déjà vu*.

Mellard, James M. "*Catch-22*: *Déjà vu* and the Labyrinth of Memory." *Bucknell Review* 16 (1968): 29–44. Argues that *déjà vu* relates not only to the social theme and Yossarian's personal problems, but also to a "universal myth, the myth of journey into the underworld."

Merrill, Robert. "The Structure and Meaning of *Catch-22*." *Studies in American Fiction* 14 (1986): 139–52. A reconsideration of Heller's technique and message in *Catch-22*.

Miller, Wayne Charles. "Ethic Identity as Moral Focus: A Reading of Joseph Heller's *Good as Gold*." *MELUS* 6 (1979): 3–17. Rpt. Nagel, *Critical Essays on Joseph Heller*. The best discussion of *Good as Gold*, though a bit enthusiastic in its praise.

Milne, Victor J. "Heller's 'Bologniad': A Theological Perspective on *Catch-22*." *Critique* 12 (1970): 50–69. Claims that in the conclusion of the novel Yossarian and the chaplain "discard their vision of the pagan universe of the epic for Christian faith in a God of salvation."

Monk, Donald. "An Experiment in Therapy: A Study of *Catch-22*." *The London Review* 2 (1967): 12–19. Sees the world of *Catch-22* as a microcosm of an insane modern world in which Yossarian is forced to make a separate peace.

Muste, John M. "Better to Die Laughing: The War Novels of Joseph Heller and John Ashmead." *Critique* 5 (1962): 16–27. Places Heller and Ashmead in a tradition which treats war as essentially humorous.

Nagel, James. "*Catch-22* and Angry Humor: A Study of the Normative Values of Satire." *Studies in American Humor* 1 (1974): 99–106. An intelligent, thoroughgoing attempt to read *Catch-22* as a traditional satire.

Nelson, Thomas Allen. "Theme and Structure in *Catch-22*." *Renascence* 23 (1971): 173–82. One of the better earlier studies of the novel's "cyclical" structure.

Bibliography

Olderman, Raymond M. "The Grail Knight Departs." *Beyond the Waste Land: The American Novel of the Nineteen-Sixties.* New Haven: Yale University Press, 1972. 94–116. An early discussion of the meanings of *Catch-22*.

Pinsker, Sanford. "Heller's *Catch-22:* The Protest of the *Puer Eternis.*" *Critique* 7 (1965): 150–62. Sees Yossarian as the typical American picaresque hero and *Catch-22* as a forerunner of the novel of the absurd.

Podhoretz, Norman. "The Best Catch There Is." *Doings and Undoings.* New York: Farrar, Strauss, 1964. 228–35. Sees Yossarian as a "youthful idealist" who becomes disillusioned with the corruption of his world. Podhoretz also takes issue with the conclusion of the novel, finding it weak and inconsistent with the previous action.

Protherough, Robert. "The Sanity of *Catch-22*." *The Human World* 3 (1971): 59–70. A discussion of the novel's satiric devices.

Ramsey, Vance. "From Here to Absurdity: Heller's *Catch-22*." *Seven Contemporary Authors: Essays on Cozzens, Miller, Golding, Heller, Albee, and Powers.* Ed. Thomas P. Whitbread. Austin: University of Texas Press, 1966. 97–118. Argues that the themes and technique of Heller's novels are within the tradition of the theater of the absurd.

Richter, David H. "The Achievement of Shape in Twentieth-Century Fable: Joseph Heller's *Catch-22*." *Fable's End: Completeness and Closure in Rhetorical Fiction.* Chicago: University of Chicago Press, 1974. 136–65. The best single essay on *Catch-22*. Identifies the book as an apologue and clarifies Heller's fictional method.

Ritter, Jesse. "Fearful Comedy: *Catch-22* as Avatar of the Social Surrealist Novel." *A Catch-22 Casebook*, ed. Kiley and McDonald. 73–86. Discusses the structure of *Catch-22* from the perspective of the modern ironic mode, the social surrealist novel.

Rudderman, Judith. "Upside-Down in *Good as Gold:* Moishe Kapoyer as Muse." *Yiddish* 5 (1984): 55–63. An intelligent case for the specifically jewish commitments of *Good as Gold*.

Searles, George J. "*Something Happened:* A New Direction for Joseph Heller." *Critique* 18 (1977): 74–81. The first important essay on *Something Happened*. Argues that the novel is superior to *Catch-22*.

Seltzer, Leon F. "Milo's 'Culpable Innocence': Absurdity as Moral Insanity in *Catch-22*." *Papers on Language and Literature* 15 (1979):

Bibliography

290–310. Rpt. Nagel, *Critical Essays on Joseph Heller*. The best discussion of Milo's and Heller's treatment of capitalism in general.

Solomon, Eric. "From Christ in Flanders to *Catch-22:* An Approach to War Fiction." *Texas Studies in Literature and Language* 11 (1969): 851–66. Places *Catch-22* in the tradition of war fiction. Sees Yossarian as a mock Christ figure.

Solomon, Jan. "The Structure of Joseph Heller's Catch-22." *Critique* 9 (1967): 46–57.

Sniderman, Stephen L. " 'It Was All Yossarian's Fault': Power and Responsibility in *Catch-22.*" *Twentieth Century Literature* 19 (1973): 251–58. Rpt. Nagel, *Critical Essays on Joseph Heller*. The first essay to direct our full attention to Yossarian's complicity in the novel's evils. The charges against Yossarian are exaggerated, however.

Strehle, Susan. " 'A Permanent Game of Excuses': Determinism in Heller's *Something Happened*." *Modern Fiction Studies* 24 (1978–79): 550–56. Rpt. Nagel, *Critical Essays on Joseph Heller*. A crucial essay that identifies Heller's thematic concern as the dangers of rationalization. Extreme, though, in its claim that Slocum deliberately murders his son.

Tanner, Tony. *City of Words: American Fiction 1950–1970*. London: Cape, 1971. 72–84. Argues that *Catch-22* is really about the "struggle for survival of the individual within his own society." Yossarian's enemy is American society manifested in the military.

Tucker, Lindsey. "Entropy and Information Theory in Heller's *Something Happened*." *Contemporary Literature* 25 (Fall 1984): 323–40.

Wain, John. "A New Novel about Old Troubles." *Critical Quarterly* 5 (1963): 168–73. Sees Yossarian as a modern hero, a character who strives toward an ideal but who is doomed to failure in a corrupt world.

Walden, Daniel. " 'Therefore Choose Life': A Jewish Interpretation of Heller's *Catch-22*." Nagel, *Critical Essays on "Catch-22."* 57–63. A brief but eloquent formulation of Heller's affirmative message in *Catch-22*.

Waldmeir, Joseph J. *American Novels of the Second World War*. The Hague: Mouton, 1969. 160–65. Places *Catch-22* in a tradition which sees war as absurd. Questions Yossarian's prowar statements near the end as unconvincing.

Bibliography

Way, Brian. "Formal Experiment and Social Discontent: Joseph Heller's *Catch-22*." *Journal of American Studies* 2 (1968): 253–70. An important essay that exaggerates Heller's connections with the theater of the absurd but identifies his ties with the American naturalists.

Index

Index

Index

Index

Index

Index

Index